The Sweet Spot

Great Golf Starts Here

2017 Edition

Three ESSENTIAL Keys

To

Control, Consistency and Power

Geoff Greig

PGA Teaching Professional

TABLE OF CONTENTS

PUBLISHERS NOTES

Disclaimer

This publication is intended to provide helpful and informative material for golfers seeking to improve their skill level and have more fun playing the game.

The author and publisher specifically disclaim all responsibility for any liability, loss or risk, personal or otherwise, which is incurred as a consequence, directly or indirectly, from the use or application of any contents of this book.

DEDICATION

If you have ever...

Stood over a golf shot and known that your golf ball would not end up anywhere near your target... and you had no idea why.

Found THE key to your golf swing only to discover it did not work the next day or even the next shot... and you had no idea why.

Tried to improve your golf swing... only to be frustrated by old swing flaws that ignore your best efforts to make them go away.

This book is dedicated to you.

I wrote The Sweet Spot to show you the "Keys" to *Sweet Spot Shots*.

The "Keys" that will help you clearly visualize THE *essential swing movements*... and how they produce *Sweet Spot Shots*.

The "Keys" that will help you simplify the process of *diagnosing* your golf shots so you can *accurately* assess exactly *what* you need to change... for *your* swing to produce *Sweet Spot Shots* consistently.

The "Keys" that will help you take THE *essential swing movements* and *accurate ball flight diagnosis* and clearly understand *how* to apply them... to *tune your swing* to start hitting more targets and playing better golf on the course.

Once you understand the dynamics of the "Keys" and how they relate to *your* swing you can start making positive changes... by following the proven and tested Sweet Spot training methods created to adapt *your* swing to execute the "Keys".

The words and pictures in The Sweet Spot are designed to be a *starting point* for you to begin developing a swing you can trust... a swing that feels good and works even better.

Once you clearly understand and accurately train The Sweet Spot "Keys" presented in this book... you can take your swing and your game to even higher levels using my 30 lesson Sweet Spot Shots Video Series.

My hope is that you find the information in this book simple to understand, easy to integrate into your golf swing and helpful in achieving your golfing goals.

You may notice that I mention a few concepts in this book multiple times and in multiple sections. These concepts are game changers... so please forgive the repetition. Hopefully it makes it easier to remember the things that will help *your* swing create more Sweet Spot Shots.☺

Geoff

INTRODUCTION

Swinging a golf club can produce very frustrating results.

A great shot one swing... a terrible shot the next swing.

Every golfer at every skill level... has had to play through this confidence deflating experience.

Improving your golf swing can be equally as frustrating.

If you do not know exactly **what** to fix in *your* swing AND the most effective steps **how** to fix it... you can invest a lot of time and energy and not improve at all.

I wrote The Sweet Spot to help you **simplify** the **what** and **clarify** the **how**.

Simplifying the **what**... means the content of this book will be focusing on just the ***essential swing movements*** that have the most influence on where your golf ball flies. There is a staggering volume of swing concepts and improvement tips available... we will only focus on the pieces of the swing puzzle that will give your improvement program the best results for the least amount of effort possible.

Clarifying the **how**... means I will show you ***Progressions*** that clearly outline your "step by step" improvement process. Changing *movement patterns* is not a one-step process. It is a *sequence* of tested and proven steps that will help you make the changes quickly and keep the old habits from returning.

The first *Progression* I recommend that you use to speed your improvement process is... the "Sweet Spot Shots" *Progression*.

The "Sweet Spot Shots" *Progression* is a three-step *conceptual* process that will take you from understanding the "Keys" of what controls ball flight... to relating these "Keys" to the *essential swing movements* of *your* swing... to a complete description of the *process* you will use to make the changes.

Before you begin making a *physical* change to your swing it is very important you have a *clear* mental *image* of what your Club Face change will be, how your body will move differently and what the basic process is to quickly and permanently make the change. Have you ever seen a tip on TV or read a tip online and gone straight to the range to test it out? How much success did you have? Did it work for a while and then mysteriously stop working? Did it work for a while and then another issue came along so you forgot all about the original tip? Maybe it did not work at all... even though it made perfect sense in your mind. **Why is this such a common occurrence? Because merely focusing on a new movement does not mean it will magically become the new *pattern/habit* for *your* swing.**

Following the "Sweet Spot Shots" *Progression* is step one in making a permanent change to *your* golf swing.

Here is the "Sweet Spot Shots" Progression":

1. *Club Face Impact Keys*
2. *Direct Influences on the Club Face*
3. *How to Make Changes*

Club Face Impact Keys

If you want your shots to fly to your targets... you need to train your swing to execute three *Club Face Keys* at Impact.

THREE THINGS... that is all.

Create correct loft on the Club Face... Face **Loft**

Swing the Club Face toward the target at impact... Face **Path**

Square the Club Face as late as possible before... Face **Aim**

Clearly understanding these three "Keys" is the starting point for you making positive changes and following the "Sweet Spot Shots" *Progression*.

When you perform these three things correctly... they will make sure you strike the ball on the Sweet Spot and send your shots to your targets.

Correct Face **Loft** at Impact will help you eliminate fat, thin and topped shots and helps you start to tune the distance and trajectory that each of your clubs will fly.

Correct Face **Path** at Impact will help you minimize slice spin and hook spin, will help you make contact on the middle of the Club Face and will also give you the most *ball speed* at impact relative to your swing speed.

Correct Face **Aim** at Impact will make sure your shots start their flight in the same direction that you are swinging your Club Face. It also helps optimize trajectory and helps minimize curvature at the end of your shots.

You may have noticed each of these *Keys* occurs at Impact.

Impact is the moment of truth for your golf swing.

It is the fraction of a second that determines where your golf ball will end up... every time you swing.

Everything you do in your swing from addressing the ball to your finish position... is only important for how it influences what your Club Face is doing at Impact.

The *Club Face Impact Keys* are the difference between your best shots and the shots you wish you could wipe from your memory banks. They are the difference between your swing and the swings you see on television producing amazing shots that you wish you could experience... and repeat!

Understanding and training these the *Club Face Impact Keys* will help you produce more *Sweet Spot Shots*... without having to reconstruct your entire golf swing. There are lots of parts to the golf swing and all of them have an influence on your shots. But you will see the best results from the least amount of change... by focusing on the *Club Face Impact Keys*.

The bottom line is... you can do anything you want with any part of your swing. If the *Club Face Impact Keys* and the "quality of the strike" are correct... you have control of your golf shots.

<u>*Direct Influences on the Club Face*</u>

When you want more *Sweet Spot Shots*... you need to train your Club Face to execute the *Club Face Impact Keys* correctly.

The most effective way to change your Club Face movement to execute the *Club Face Impact Keys* ... is to change the movement of the part of your body that has the most "Direct Influence" on the Club Face.

One of my goals in this book is to help you identify, clarify and train the most "Direct Influences" on ball flight... so you can make the least amount of change and get the most powerful results.

- The Club Face is the only "Direct Influence" on the flight of the Ball
- The Guiding Hand is the most "Direct Influence" on the Club Face

My recommendation is to focus on training the Club Face and the Guiding Hand... for utmost efficiency and speed in the process of improving your *Club Face Impact Keys*.

The Guiding Hand (the lower hand on the grip) is the closest part of your body to the Club Face, which means it is your "Direct Influence" (control) of the Club Face... it also gives you a very accurate sense for the movement of the Club Face.

Accurate awareness of Club Face movement at Impact is one of the most powerful tools you have for improving the quality of your swing and your shots.

It is very important to remember this Club Face focus/awareness should be limited to when you are training your swing at the range... not performing on the course.

Thinking about **any** movements in your swing while you are playing golf on the course... is like thinking about the movements of your wrist and your fingers while writing your signature. You will get an ugly looking signature.

When you want a "pretty" signature you focus on the *goal* (a "pretty" signature), not on the *process* (the moving pieces that write the signature).

The same is true for your golf swing.

If you want "pretty" shots, focus on the *goal*... the target. Do not focus on the *process*... the moving parts.

Focusing on the *process* is effective for training the moving parts... but not effective for achieving your *goal* of hitting the target.

Use your brain/focus to closely monitor your moving parts during the training process to make sure you are training effective and accurate movements.

When it is time to hit the target on the course... focus your brain on the target and trust your body to perform the way you have trained it.

How to Make Changes

The fastest and most effective way to integrate correct *Club Face Impact Keys* into your swing and train your "Direct Influences" on the Club Face to happen accurately and consistently... is to follow two basic guidelines:

Minimum Change –

- **Change only what is necessary for you to achieve your effective *Club Face Impact Keys*.** Attempting to change too many things is a recipe for frustration and failure.
- **Correct "Direct Influences" First.** The concept of "Direct Influences" is a very important piece of *minimizing* the amount of change you need to implement to achieve efficient *Club Face Impact Keys*.

Maximum Results –

- **Relate all swing changes to how they affect your *Club Face Impact Keys*.** This will guarantee that time spent practicing... is spent on the essential changes that have a powerful and "Direct Influence" on your shots.
- **Follow the "Learning" *Progression*.** The "Learning" *Progression* is the second *Progression* we will use and it is the main tool for making the *physical* changes to how you swing the Club Face.

The "Learning" *Progression is:*

- Clearly Visualize the movements you desire (**See**)
- Accurately match your movements to the Visual (**Feel**)
- Perform correct repetitions to create a pattern (**Train)**
- Execute successful challenges to the pattern (**Trust**)

I have tested and tuned the "Learning" *Progression* on my own swing and with my students... to produce the fastest *swing pattern change* with the least amount of repetitions.

Discipline yourself to follow the "Learning" *Progression* **like you would implement a business plan for a new business. This will give you a "step by step" change map for any change you want to make in your golf swing or golf game.**

There are no "hidden secrets" or "perfect swings" in the game of golf. The pros all swing differently... so can you.

Your source for success... is to train your Club Face to move through Impact correctly and send the ball to the target consistently and efficiently. Even if your swing is unique, unconventional or unorthodox... if your Club Face is moving correctly at Impact your shots will fly to your targets.

Training correct movement of the Club Face means you MUST first become aware of what correct movement *FEELS* **like... compared to what incorrect movement** *FEELS* **like.**

If you can't *feel* **the difference... your practice is merely reinforcing old/bad swing habits.**

Focusing on the Club Face movement at Impact is not a revolutionary concept. All effective instructors help their students create correct Club Face movement at Impact.

Focusing on the Guiding Hand however... is *Evolutionary*. Most instructors teach that controlling the Club Face with the hands is unreliable. When playing on the course... this can be true.

But... the hands are a great source of accurate *FEEL*.

Since the first step to creating effective Club Face movement is accurately *FEELING* the difference between correct and incorrect... a comfortable source of *feel* is crucial to your success.

My students have found Guiding Hand *feel* to be a great *starting place* for improving the awareness of Club Face movement and what their personal "good swing" *feels* like.

Once you have raised your awareness of *correct versus incorrect*... you can then begin to discover what part of your body is best for you to *focus* on when executing your shots on the course. I have seen effective performance *focus* vary from hands... to arms... to shoulders... to chest... to core... to hips... and even legs or feet.

The chapter breakdown of The Sweet Spot is structured to follow the **Minimum Change/Maximum Results** guidelines.

If you do your best to follow these guidelines in your practice... you will dramatically increase your probability of success.

It is also important that you keep in mind the *"Essential Elements"* of *Sweet Spot Shots* while you are training the *"Club Face Impact Keys"* of *swing improvement.*

"Essential Elements" of Sweet Spot Shots

Ball... Club Face... Target

- **Strike the Sweet Spot of the Ball.**
- **With the Sweet Spot of the Club Face.**
- **With your *focus* on the Target.**

These may seem to be unrealistically simple concepts... especially since the golf swing is a complicated movement sequence with lots of moving body parts.

But, if the *"Club Face Impact Keys"* of *swing improvement* and the *"Essential Elements"* of *Sweet Spot Shots* are the *driving force* behind all your change goals... you will be much less likely to get lost in the vast databases of golf swing "pieces and parts" knowledge that is readily available in today's information (overload) society.

I strongly recommend you focus on "accurately training" one *Club Face Impact Key* at a time.

One of the primary causes of determined and dedicated golfers failing to improve is understanding multiple new concepts and not fully training any of them. It is often called "Paralysis from Analysis". A head full of ideas... and a body confused by too many commands from the brain. Have you experienced this before?

Before you can put these *Club Face Impact Key* dynamics to work in your *swing improvement* program and accomplish successful *"Essential Elements"* of *Sweet Spot Shots*... you need to ask yourself a few questions:

1. **Do you know exactly where the Sweet Spot of the Ball is?**
2. **Do you know exactly where the Sweet Spot of each Club Face is?**
3. **Do you know the most effective way to Guide the Club Face to consistently connect the Sweet Spots and launch your shots to the target?**

There are a LOT of pieces to the puzzle of playing better golf.

Which means it is very important to **"tune in your *focus*"** on what can help you most... especially if you want to make the most efficient use of your practice time.

Fully understanding AND training the three *Club Face Impact Keys* in your practice will guarantee you get Maximum Results from Minimum Change... and help you unlock the true potential of your swing.

Focusing on the three *"Essential Elements"* of *Sweet Spot Shots* during your play and your target oriented practice, will guarantee you "lock in" to your targets so you do not get lost in the swing process... and help you unlock the true potential of your on-course play.

This book is the culmination of 20 years of teaching experience and swing research... *reduced* to the most *essential swing movements* and proven improvement *Progressions*. It is specifically designed to give you:

- **Universal "Key" Impact Concepts**
- **Powerful Swing Training Exercises**
- **Helpful Hints for Accurate Self Diagnosis**

For a book whose pages contain few words, The Sweet Spot has a lot of important information to explore on each page.

I strongly recommend taking your time to study each concept in depth... and learn to *feel* the difference between correct and incorrect movements in your practice... to maximize your learning experience and achieve the most powerful results.

In other words, create a "*clear picture*" of each new concept in your mind and experience the correct "*feel*" of each new movement with your body... before moving on to the next concept.

A clear and accurate awareness of what it *looks* like and *feels* like when your Club Face moves correctly in the *Release Zone*... is a powerful step in your success process.

Essentially, use the "**Learning**" *Progression* to get the most out of this book.

My students who progress the fastest... practice a lot of "visualizations" of new swing movements and perform a lot of "eyes closed" training swings... to clarify the image of their Sweet Spot swing and to heighten their sense of feel for that swing.

No golf ball. No target. Just daily rehearsal swings in front of a mirror and then with their eyes closed... to increase their **awareness of correct versus incorrect** *picture* and *feel*.

Dedicating *all* your practice time to hitting balls at the range... is a great example of Einstein's definition of insanity. You are essentially doing to same thing you have always done... and expecting a different result. No matter how strongly you are *focusing* on making a new movement when hitting balls at the range... in the beginning part of the change process, your body is "wired" to execute your old swing pattern.

It is ok to hit balls at the range early in the change process... but make sure you are doing at least 4 or 5 correct practice swings in between every shot with a golf ball. This will make sure you are getting a much higher percentage of accurate "new" swings... and thus speeding the change process.

Hitting balls at the range will most certainly help you gain confidence in a new movement and get ready for the course... but only once you can *accurately* feel the difference between right and wrong in every swing.

CHAPTER 1- THE SWEET SPOT

Extraordinary golf shots.

Always vivid in your golfing memories.

They look different... soaring higher, farther and truer.

They feel different... as if the ball weighed nothing when your club struck it.

They inspire you... to wake early for your next round or practice late to capture the experience again.

The Sweet Spot shot is much more than just another stroke on the scorecard and more than just a dream... that only the tour pros achieve.

The Sweet Spot shot is also your perfect blueprint for rapid improvement and sustained excellence.

Golf is a target game. Pick a target for every shot.

Train your swing... to send your shots to your target.

Golfers who play the best and have the most fun... hit their targets more often than everyone else. Some hit longer shots, some hit shorter shots, some hit higher shots, some hit lower shots... but good players hit more targets with whatever shot they can consistently execute.

When I do playing lessons with new students I always ask... "What is your target for this shot?" It never ceases to amaze me how many times the answer is vague (the whole fairway or the entire green) or negative (anywhere but the trees). Have you listened to the dialogue between tour players and their caddies? They are picking VERY **specific positive targets**. Even if with their million dollar swings, they know they will not hit the exact target every time.

Playing better golf is "theoretically" as simple as picking the right target and hitting your shot to the target. The reality is... we will not hit our precise targets very often. But without picking a precise target for every shot... you are not giving your brain and your swing the information it needs to succeed.

Sweet Spot shots are the most powerful, the most consistent and the most efficient way to hit more *Sweet Spot Shots* and hit more targets.

If you ever have a chance... look at the face of a PGA Tour Professional's clubs.

If the clubs are not brand new... you will see a worn spot right in the Sweet Spot of the club. All tour pros hit virtually all their shots on the Sweet Spot.

If you have unlimited time, energy, money and patience please feel free to attempt to build a "perfect swing" piece by piece... as a means to hitting more targets.

But remember... each small change you make to your swing will take a **minimum** of three weeks before it begins to work effectively on the course.

The Change Process

If you want to start hitting more targets RIGHT NOW and use your current swing to do it... Sweet Spot Shots are your most direct path to Success.

The best players in the world all have different swings. Upright, flat, quick, smooth, simple, complex... no two great swings are alike.

The reason they are the best players is because their swing Impacts the Sweet Spot of the Club Face on the Sweet Spot of the golf ball... and their shots hit their targets. Not because they have "perfect swings".

It is the *Effectiveness* of your swing that matters... not the *Style* of your swing.

A Sweet Spot swing is an *Effective* swing that connects the Sweet Spots on the Club Face and the Ball, executes the Club Face Impact Keys... and sends the ball to the target.

The *"Essential Elements"* that produce *Sweet Spot Shots* also provide the guidelines for creating a Sweet Spot *Effective* swing:

1. **Strike the Sweet Spot of the Ball**
2. **With the Sweet Spot of the Club Face**
3. **Moving accurately in the Release Zone**

The only "Direct Influence" on your Ball Flight is your Club Face. When your Club Face strikes the ball correctly in the Impact area of the *Release Zone...* your shots will hit your targets no matter what the rest of your swing *looks* like.

The most "Direct Influence" on the Club Face is your Guiding Hand (the lower hand on the club). Your Guiding Hand is the closest part of your body to the Club Face and this gives you direct control and a high degree of awareness of the Club Face movement.

The golf ball does not know what your feet, legs, hips, core, shoulders and elbows are doing.

It only reacts to the Club Face movements and Club Face contact in the Release Zone.

For example: if you focus on moving your hips differently it may or may not create the desired effect in your Club Face movement at Impact.

This is because movements of the hips must translate through the core, shoulders, arms and hands before they get to the Club Face.

Thus, the hips are an Indirect Influence on Club Face movement at Impact.

I am not saying that your feet, legs, your hips, your core, your shoulders and your elbows are not important.

They all play a role in helping you hit more targets.

But, the most Direct Influence on you hitting more targets... is the Club Face and the part of your body that directly *guides* the Club Face.

The **Release Zone** is the area of the swing where your Club Face moves from the height of your Guiding Hand on the downswing to the height of your Guiding Hand on the follow through. The rest of your golf swing can be adapted to match your build, strength, flexibility, age, time constraints and goals.

If your Guiding Hand and the Club Face are moving accurately and efficiently in the *Release Zone*, you can execute the rest of your swing in way that feels comfortable for you... and you will consistently hit Sweet Spot shots to your target.

In my experience working with students, focusing their improvement process on this area of the swing has yielded tremendous results. It has helped them simplify what they need to focus on in their practice and minimize what they need to diagnose when they are playing on the course.

Keeping focus simple and making diagnostics easier means you can spend less time thinking about what to do... and spend more time *seeing* and *feeling* how to do it.

When interacting with new students, it always amazes me how much information they attempt to process regarding; weight transfer, hip rotation, shoulder plane, spine tilt, shaft angle etc. etc. etc. Many even attempt to process all these thoughts *every swing*.

Unfortunately, very few know the exact location of the Sweet Spot on the ball and on the Club Face. Fewer still know the optimum *Release Zone* movement of the Guiding Hand and the Club Face.

That is like owning a Ferrari and knowing the complete workings of an internal combustion engine but, not knowing where the key goes and how the steering wheel works. Sweet Spot Contact is your ignition key and *Release Zone* Movement is your steering wheel.

Since Sweet Spot contact and *Release Zone* movement of the Club Face and Guiding Hand are the only "Direct Influences" on your shots... it makes sense to understand them FULLY and change them first.

"Direct Influences" produce Immediate, Powerful, Positive Change with accurate practice... Indirect Influences may never produce the desired change.

Think of your swing like a business. If want to generate more sales for your "business", would you create a marketing campaign that attracts more people to your product... or would you do an audit of office expenses? "Direct Influences" are the most direct route to positive changes.

To rapidly improve *your* "Direct Influences" make sure to follow the *Learning Progression*...

- Create the correct picture *in your mind* of *Release Zone* movement and connecting the Sweet Spots**. (See)**
- Raise your awareness of the difference in *FEEL in your body* between correct and incorrect movements. **(Feel)**
- Do at least 80% of your swings correctly (they may need to be practice swings at first) to groove the new swing pattern. **(Train)**
- Challenge yourself to execute the new movements in progressively more "game like" situations while maintaining the 80% success guideline. **(Trust)**

It is very important to remember that focusing on "Direct Influences" is a PRACTICE/TRAINING TOOL... to help you become aware of what is not ideal in your swing and to LEARN how to change it.

Let me repeat that for emphasis...

Focusing on parts of your body and specific movements/positions in your swing can be powerful *training tools*... but they are not effective *performance* tools. This book is dedicated to *training* your swing to execute the *Club Face Impact Keys*.

If you want more *on course* performance tools and mental tips... my Sweet Spot Shots Video Series on Amazon Video Direct contains 5 video lessons specifically designed to help you learn how to take your best swings to the course.

Sweet Spot Simple Tip

The best way to improve positions in your swing is to do "snapshot" rehearsal/practice swings.

*The picture above... is me at the end of the Release Zone. Visualizing yourself making a full swing **through** this position to a perfect finish... is an example of a good training rehearsal "snapshot".*

Have you ever noticed tour pros stopping in certain positions during rehearsal swings? They are creating a clear picture of an important position "snapshot" in a rehearsal/practice swing... and then trusting their body to recreate this position when they swing with a ball to the target.

Use "snapshot" rehearsals in practice/practice swings to build trust in your positions... so you can focus on the target when you are hitting shots to targets.

CHAPTER 2- THE GOLF BALL

Your shots can find their way to the target via any number of paths, some more pleasing to the eye (and the ego) than others. You may have already experienced this.

A giant slice can still manage to find the fairway just like a low, thin iron shot can still end up on the green.

However, the greatest enjoyment happens when your shots are *Sweet Spot Shots* and they match the picture in your mind's eye. Experiencing these shots with more consistency is an achievable goal and hopefully will be the fuel to motivate you to do daily training/rehearsal swings.

If you want maximum control, consistency and power from your swing... then learning to introduce the Sweet Spot of the Club Face to the Sweet Spot of the ball is the first step toward achieving your goal.

You will be amazed at how quickly your body will adapt the rest of your swing to correct flawed movement patterns... simply by giving it an accurate and correct picture of Sweet Spot Impact for each swing.

For example: If you know what your signature looks like... even if the pen is an odd shape and your arm is at slightly different angle than normal, you can probably still write a signature that is recognizable.

This is because you have a clear picture in your mind of what your signature looks like (and you have done it a few thousand times).

The same can be true for your golf swing.

Develop a clear picture of correct Impact and practice that Impact "snapshot" on a consistent basis and the current flaws in your swing related to that picture... will begin to re-pattern themselves.

You may have a few stubborn patterns/flaws that will require extra attention but creating a clear, correct picture of Sweet Spot Shot Impact for *your* swing... will save you a lot of time in your improvement process.

Faulty weight transfers, over the top transitions, casting and scooping are just a few of the flaws that will begin to fix themselves by focusing on ideal Sweet Spot contact for each swing. For example:

- When you try to strike underneath the equator to help the ball into the air... this can cause your weight to stay on your back foot as you approach Impact.
- When your ball is slicing to the right you will often attempt to swing left of the target at impact to minimize the effect of the slice... this can cause your transition to move "over the top".
- When you are not hitting the ball as far as you would like you may start moving the club head too fast too early in the downswing... this is the blueprint for casting.

These and many other flaws are caused (at least in part) by having an incorrect image of Sweet Spot contact and *Release Zone* movement of the Club Face.

Use the *Club Face Impact Keys* to diagnose your most challenging Impact flaw. Once you understand the flaw and the ball flight issue it creates... spend a few minutes each day for a week picturing the correct movement.

The next time you go to the range to hit balls after the "visualization" week you may be very surprised at the changes in your swing. **Try it!**

When you connect the Sweet Spots... you optimize backspin and minimize sidespin.

Every golf shot that stays in the air has backspin.

Optimizing backspin means you will achieve the ideal balance between the distance the ball flies, the trajectory it flies on and how quickly it stops.

Spin rates can range from roughly 2000 rpm with the driver to over 10,000 rpm with the wedges. Don't worry there will not be any pop quizzes on spin rates.

What you do need to remember is... striking the Equator of the golf ball gives you the best chance of creating maximum compression and optimum backspin for whatever club you are swinging.

Minimizing sidespin means straighter shots... which will help keep your drives in the fairway and your irons on the green.

We will go into more detail about sidespin in the next chapter.

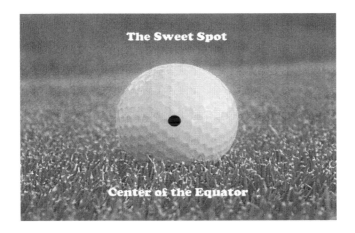

The Equator

THE Spot for Optimum Backspin

Would you like to eliminate shots where your club digs in to the ground before it hits the ball... or shots where the bottom of your club hits the top of the ball and it rolls down the fairway?

Solid contact, optimized backspin and maximum compression for most full swing shots is only achieved when your Club Face strikes the equator of the ball.

Whenever the Club Face strikes above or below the equator, less than ideal spin rates are created and distance and compression are reduced. The farther you strike above the equator, the greater chance there is of creating topspin and topped shots. The farther you strike below the equator, the more you add loft to the Club Face and subtract distance. You also dramatically increase the chance of contacting ground before you strike the ball. **Again... striking the equator creates optimum compression, spin rate and trajectory.**

33

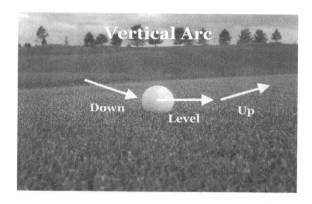

The Vertical Club Face Arc (Loft at Impact)

The most "Direct Influence" on whether you strike the equator of the ball is the Vertical Arc of your Club Face. Each time you swing a golf club in the *Release Zone* there are three parts to the Vertical Arc of the swing:

Moving Downward/Level/Moving Upward

The Vertical Club Face Arc is not only the most "Direct Influence" on your ability to strike the equator of the ball... it is also the most Direct Influence on correct Club Face Loft at Impact. Another way to think about the Vertical Arc is... where does the low point/bottom of your golf swing occur. Good players have a VERY small window of where their club swing arc "bottoms out" from swing to swing. More about the precise placement of the "bottom" coming up soon.

The "Key" is... I want to help you train your swing to "bottom out" (reach its low point) in a place that will give you consistently solid contact of the Sweet Spot of your Club Face on the Sweet Spot of the ball.

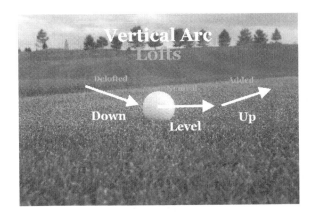

When your Club Face is moving downward the Club Face is de-lofted.

When your Club Face is moving level the Club Face is neutral lofted.

When the Club Face is moving upward your Club Face has added loft.

Each of the three parts of the Vertical Arc can be useful at impact... with certain clubs on certain swings.

Short/Mid Irons – De-Lofted.

Hybrids/Fairway Woods – De-Lofted or Neutral Lofted

Driver – Neutral lofted/Slight Added Loft

Let's start by creating an accurate visual of the ideal Vertical Arc approaches of the Club Face to promote equator contact... with each of the different club groups:

Irons

When the ball is resting on the ground... the club should be travelling slightly downward with the irons to consistently strike the equator of the ball on the Sweet Spot of the iron and create ideal Loft on the Club Face. This means your Club Face will be de-lofted and the ball will be struck before the turf is contacted when swinging irons. **The phrase to remember is... "hit the little ball (the golf ball) and then the big ball (the earth).**

The turf contact should start where the middle of the ball was resting... in most cases the middle of your stance. For simplicity and consistency, I recommend putting the ball in the middle of your stance for all your short and mid iron shots. This way you do not have to change where your swing "bottoms out" for each different club group.

Remember... the lowest part of the Vertical Arc is always in front of the ball (towards the target) with a Sweet Spot iron swing.

Hybrids and Fairway Woods

With hybrids or fairway woods a slightly downward Vertical Arc is best. However, a level approach will work if the ball is sitting up or if you are striving for a higher trajectory. Place the ball one to two inches in front of the middle of your stance (with a slightly wider stance) to create the shallower approach and allow the Club Face to reach a less de-lofted position.

The Club Face will still be slightly de-lofted on the slightly downward swing (one inch forward of center ball position) and neutral lofted when the Club Face is moving level to the ground at impact (two inches forward of center ball position).

The lowest part of the Vertical Arc is still in front of the ball with most hybrids/fairway woods shots... as with the irons. The approach will be slightly shallower (less turf will be scuffed after impact) because the added length of the club shafts means that you must stand farther from the ball creating a flatter swing plane.

On the Tee with Irons and Hybrids

With the ball teed up, the lowest part of the Vertical Arc can be at or in front of the ball.

When the lowest part of the arc is *at the ball* you will create sweeping (level) contact and a neutral lofted Club Face... which will launch the ball on a high trajectory for maximum carry distance and soft landings but with slightly less backspin.

When the lowest part of the arc is slightly *in front of the ball* you will create a trapping (downward) impact and a de-lofted Club Face... which produces a lower trajectory and added backspin for more directional control.

Be careful about teeing the ball too high with these clubs (more than ½ inch) ... striking the ball high on the Club Face can cause shots to come up short of your target.

Woods on the Tee

With the fairway woods and driver on a tee, a level approach is best for control. This creates the ideal combination of launch angle, trajectory and spin rate for accurate drives.

A slightly upward approach is effective with the driver... if you are seeking a higher launch for more carry distance and less spin.

You can use ball position and tee height to help change your angle of approach with the driver. Forward ball position (opposite the front foot arch) and high tee height promote a slightly upward approach. Move the ball position back an inch or two and use a lower tee for a level sweep and more control.

The most common cause of missing the equator of the ball is attempting to get the Club Face "underneath" the equator of the ball with your swing... and "help" it into the air. This can happen with all clubs but, it is most common with the irons. If I only had a dollar for every time I have heard someone say... "I didn't get under the ball." *When the ball is resting on the ground... the goal is to "trap" the ball or "sweep" the ball off the ground.*

Striking below the equator and trying to add loft to the club can cause ground first contact (where the divot often flies further than the ball), topped shots and it also minimizes desired backspin.

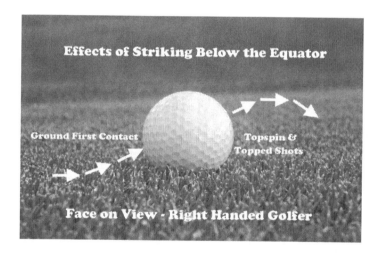

Attempting to help the ball in the air, (scooping/adding loft) also causes problems in the body (reverse weight shift at impact and "chicken wing" left arm after impact being the most common). **The easiest way to fix the contact issues AND the body issues is to...**

Change Your Mental Picture

Your *Effective* <u>Mental Swing Picture</u> is to visualize your swing propelling the ball "forward" and letting the Loft on the Club Face take care of the "up". Picture a "trap" (downward) or a "sweep" (level) motion through impact to guarantee the best contact. When you "trap" or "sweep" you allow the design of the Club Face to do its job... clubs are designed with specific amounts of Loft to produce optimum flight.

When you try to "help" the ball into the air you are adding excessive Loft to the club... making it very difficult for the Sweet Spot of the Club Face to contact the Sweet Spot of the ball and for the Loft to do its job.

This is especially true if the ball is sitting in very short grass or on firm turf. Have you ever experienced challenges in making solid contact on "tight lies"? Trying to help the ball up may be the cause.

41

Trust the Loft on your Club Face to produce the correct trajectory.

I will repeat again to emphasize the importance... a slightly downward "trapping" movement with the irons on the ground and a level "sweeping" movement with the driver will help you strike the equator of the ball on a regular basis.

Notice how the club shaft leans toward the target when de-lofting the Club Face for Sweet Spot contact. Did you ever wonder about the big divots the tour players take when hitting short irons? The divots are *after* Impact and they are caused by the shaft leaning dramatically forward at Impact... causing the bottom of the swing to be significantly in front of the ball (toward the target). **We will explore the extensive benefits of forward/positive shaft lean and de-lofting your Club Face in an upcoming chapter.**

Grooving Equator Contact

Train Your "Scuff"

When the ball is resting on the ground... every swing should *Scuff* the turf (and many will take divots). If you want to strike the equator when the ball is on the ground... you must train *where* your club *Scuffs* the turf in your swing and how deep the *Scuff* is. **Ideally when you are swinging irons, hybrids and fairway woods your *Scuff* should start in the middle of your stance. The deepest part of the *Scuff* will be a couple inches after that.**

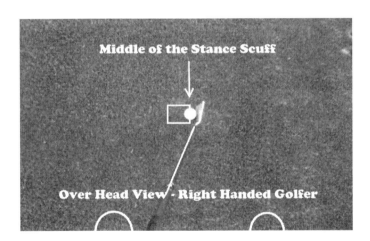

The depth and length of the *Scuff* will vary depending on which club you are swinging. Short irons will take longer, deeper *Scuffs* and fairway woods will take short, shallow *Scuffs* (sometimes only brushing the grass). **Training the placement and depth of *your* swing *Scuff* is a HUGE step forward in making Sweet Spot Contact with every club in your bag!**

Practicing a correct *Scuff* is very simple.

Find a patch of grass or sand. Place a tee opposite the middle of your stance or draw a line in the sand in the middle of your stance. Grab your favorite iron and begin swinging.

The goal is to create *Scuffs* that start exactly in the middle of your stance and are not too deep. *Scuffing* **the grass and brushing the ground lightly is sufficient until you have developed some consistency and confidence.**

Once you get consistently correct *Scuffs* without having to think about it, start trying other clubs. Generally, the 7 or 8 iron is the easiest and the long clubs and wedges are the toughest. Do NOT add a ball to the equation until correct *Scuffs* become easy, repeatable and *without thought*. **Once you start putting a ball into the equation... do your best to forget the ball and focus on the *Scuff*.**

If you get the *Scuff* right, the club design will take care of the contact, the spin and the trajectory. **A Centered *Scuff* promotes Equator Contact**.

Keeping your head centered throughout your swing can also help you keep the *Scuff* centered and consistent. The *Scuffs* do not have to be perfect but they must be close.

One half inch back of center (away from the target) is ok but *Scuffs* up to an inch and a half forward of center (toward the target) create better quality shots than *Scuffs* too far back in the stance. Forward of center *Scuffs* usually cause thin shots... thin shots still fly and may not cost you any strokes. Back of center *Scuffs* cause fat and topped shots... fat and topped shots almost always cost you a stroke.

Center of the Equator

Are you sabotaged by slices and horrified by hooks? Then learning to minimize sidespin should be at the top of your "to do" list.

Striking the center of the equator minimizes excessive sidespins (slices and hooks) and maximizes launch velocity due to increased compression of the ball at impact. It also gives you the best chance of hitting the Sweet Spot of the Club Face and being able to square the Club Face properly at Impact.

Striking the center of the equator consistently means your Club Face needs to be moving towards your target consistently at Impact. When your Club Face is moving excessively to the left or right of your target... your Impact point will move away from the center of the equator of the ball and create more sidespin on your shots.

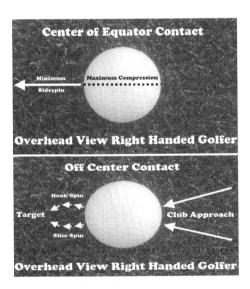

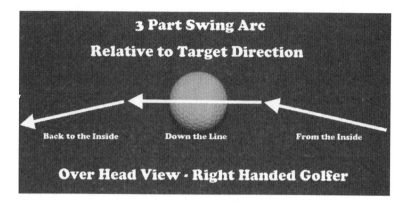

The Horizontal Club Face Arc (Path)

THE Direct Influence on Center of the Equator Contact

Consistently centered contact on the ball is only achieved when you train your Club Face to be moving in the correct Arc/Path (relative to the target) as it strikes the golf ball. There are no straight lines in full swing Club Face movement... so the key is to make sure contact is happening in the correct part of your Horizontal Club Face Arc (I will use the term "Path" for simplicity from here onward). **Just like the Vertical Arc there are three parts to the Horizontal/Target Oriented Path of each swing:**

- **Down the Line (to the target)**
- **From the Inside (to the target line)**
- **Back to the Inside (from the target line)**

Maximum distance, minimum sidespin and consistent trajectory all happen when Sweet Spot Impact occurs during the *Down the Line* part of the Path.

46

Sweet Spot Simple Tip -

If you want your ball to go to the Target with a minimum of sidespin, strike it when the Club Face is moving Down the Target Line.

Down the Line Impact is one of the few parts of the golf swing that is intuitive... and one of the parts of the swing that very few golfers execute correctly. **Every full swing, every club, strike the ball in the Down the Line part of the Path and your number of targets hit will increase dramatically... unless you purposely want to hit shots with a large amount of curvature at the end of the flight.**

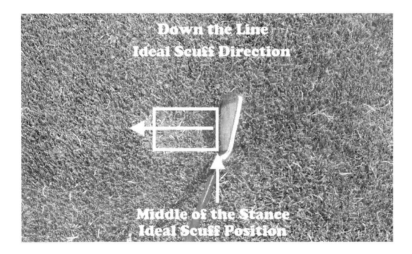

Also... now that you are Scuffing correctly, start checking your Scuffs/divots because they can help you assess your Path. If they are not going towards the target for the first couple of inches after Impact you are not contacting the ball in the correct part of your Path.

Down the Line

When the Club Face is in the *Down the Line* part of the Path, it is moving at *Maximum Speed* and that *Speed* is directed where you want your ball to end up... the Target. Miss hits will be minimized and Sweet Spot strikes will be maximized when your Club Face strikes the ball as it moves *Down the Line* to the target.

Imagine the difference between pitches in baseball. Pitchers in Major League baseball can throw fastballs up to 100 mph. The fastest curveballs rarely exceed 85 to 90 MPH.

When your Club Face is travelling *Down the Line* your shots are like Major League fastballs... minimum sidespin and maximum velocity. Your shots can still reach the target when the Club Face is in the wrong part of the Path but, controlling your distance, curvature and trajectory will be much more difficult and your consistency will suffer.

From the Inside

The Club Face moving *From the Inside* is the most forgiving of the incorrect Paths. A Club Face moving *From the Inside* is still *accelerating* and approaching the ball on a shallow (slightly downward) angle. This means you will not lose much distance and you will still have a chance to strike the ball solidly if your Club Face is moving a bit too much *From the Inside.*

***From the Inside* strikes' will most often produce contact slightly to the inside of center on the ball and below the equator which leads to high "pushes" to the right of target with minimum sidespin. These are playable misses and more importantly... predictable misses.** It is helpful to remember that the quality of your mishits (less than ideal swings/shots) is a big part of your success on the course. Good misses rarely cause big numbers on your scorecard... bad misses add strokes quickly. Like life... it is important to enjoy your good misses.

Leaving the Club Face wide open when the Club Face approaches *From the Inside* is difficult (**Try it!**), which means push slices are uncommon.

A slightly closed Club Face (relative to the target) at Impact creates the most problematic shot with the Path approaching *From the Inside*... pull hooks.

The closed Club Face (aiming left of the target) means the ball will usually start left of the target **(about 80% of the *start line* of the flight of your shots is the Club Face Aim)**

The *From the Inside Path* means the ball will tend to curve further left at the end of the flight **(the curvature at the end of the flight is a combination of Face Aim and Face Path).**

Sweet Spot Helpful Hint

When your shots are not hitting your targets... remember it is the Club Face Aim that tells the ball what direction to start its flight... and the Club Face Path that tells the ball how much to curve at the end of the flight.

Accurately diagnosing which of these is causing your issues... will help you fix things faster and with a lot less frustration.

Learning to read your *Scuffs* and read the ball flight is your most powerful tool for accurate diagnosis. It can be confusing at first... but with a little practice you will start to become your own best coach.

The big picture of minimizing mistakes with a *From the Inside* Path is just making sure the Club Face is Aiming square to slightly open... relative to the target.

By the way... a slightly *From the Inside* Path with a slightly open Club Face (aiming right of the target) is the *Release Zone* dynamic most tour pros use to produce a **draw** shape in their shots.

If you like numbers... 0-3 degrees *From the Inside* Path and .5 to 1.5-degree open Club Face is the window where most tour pro draw shots (starting slightly right and curving back to the target) come from.

It is also VERY difficult for most golfers (above single digit handicappers) to swing in a way that would bring the Club Face excessively *From the Inside* (more than 5 degrees).

I see this less than 1 swing in 100 with higher handicap golfers.

If you are one of the 1 in 100... you will see your shots flying to the right with no curve in the flight or starting to the right with a big old hook shape to the left... at the end.

In most golf swings, the direction and distance of your mistakes *From the Inside*... will be closer to those of the optimum *Down the Line* shots than shots when the Club Face is moving *Back to the Inside*.

Which reminds me of one of my favorite sayings in golf... "He or she who has the best mistakes wins".

Back to the Inside

The Club Face moving *Back to the Inside* is the least forgiving and most common of incorrect Paths.

A Club Face moving *Back to the Inside* is *decelerating* which robs you of precious distance. It will also tend to strike outside and above the equator of the golf ball in a steep downward movement often creating deep divots.

This will make consistent contact very difficult and causes both "pulled" shots long and to the left and cut/sliced shots short and to the right (for right handed golfers).

Do you notice a lot of ball marks on the toe of your Club Face? Do you notice your divots go to the left of where your target is? Do you feel like your shots always come up short of your targets? **Then you may be struggling with a Path that is moving too far *Back to the Inside*.**

In terms of different clubs...

- **Driver shots will most often slice or curve to the right when the Club Face is moving *Back to the Inside* at Impact and they will fly much shorter than a straight shot (pulls to the left can also occur).**
- **Fairway woods and hybrids will tend to look like the driver shots (with a bit less sidespin).**
- **Irons (especially short irons) will most often be high, right and short... or sometimes pulled to the left and long (depending on Face Aim).**

Both an open Club Face and a closed Club Face at Impact can be problematic with the *Back to the Inside* Path.

- Large slices happen when the Path is Back to the Inside and the Face Aim is open (relative to the target).
- Pull hooks happen when the Path is Back to the Inside and the Face Aim is closed (relative to the Path).
- Big slices and pull hooks rarely make for a fun day on the course.

This wide potential pattern of error shots/misses is what makes the *Back to the Inside* Path so troublesome.

Long and left, short and right, fat, topped... it is very difficult to pick correct targets for your shots when your mishits are in this much of a random pattern.

Ball Spotting

"The Opposite Fix" for Center of the Equator Contact

The most common Path errors I see are golfers striking the ball on the center or outside of center with the Path coming *Back to the Inside* through Impact.

The quickest way to fix this... is to learn what it feels like to strike the inside of center moving toward the outside. Once you can strike inside and outside at will... finding the middle is much easier.

"The Opposite Fix" - One of the fastest ways to break old habits and create new improved ones... is to practice doing the opposite of your current incorrect pattern.

If you have been trying to correct a mistake by attempting to do the correct movement... then all your repetitions are somewhere between your current mistake and where you want to be. **Learning to do the Opposite of your current mistake/pattern will make it much easier to start experiencing the ideal middle ground.**

There have been numerous performance studies that have concluded this "bracketing" or "*Opposite Fix*" style of learning is the most effective way to overcome a strong negative habit pattern.

Start with a 7 or 8 iron on some good turf. If you are striking the outside... your divots/scuffs will be going left through impact (for a right-handed golfer). You will most likely be hitting a dimple or more outside of center.

Your first goal is to create divots/*Scuffs* that go a bit to the outside after Impact.

Looking one dimple to the inside of center and trying to strike that spot as you extend to one dimple to the outside through impact I call... *Ball Spotting*.

There are an endless number of indirect influences that can cause you to contact the ball on the *Back to the Inside* part of the Path. You are certainly welcome to focus on shoulder alignment, hip rotation or shaft plane (to name just a few) but, you might fall prey to "Paralysis from Analysis" and never get your issue fixed.

Fix the movement of the Club Face at Impact first. It is the most Direct Influence on your ball flight.

Let your body adjust to the corrected movement of the Club Face.

If there is one "body key" my students *have* found helpful with correct Path in training... it is to picture that their shoulders are square at Impact.

Open shoulders (aiming left) tend to *pull* the Club Face *Back to the Inside*... closed shoulders (aiming right) tend to *push* the Club Face too much *From the Inside*.

Remember... as with all body cues it is important to use them as practice tools only.

Focusing on a static position in your swing can be helpful in training ("snapshots"), but it does not translate into making a full swing motion that produces good shots.

The big picture is... different players cue on different body movements to train effective Path and Centered Contact.

However, all players with Sweet Spot swings move the Club Face *Down the Line* through Impact and connect the Sweet Spots with ideal loft on the Club Face.

You may need to swing slower or smaller in the beginning to create successful Sweet Spot contact and execute the "Opposite Fix" for your swing Path.

Sweet Spot Helpful Hint

"Reduce to Produce"

If you can't create successful Path in a full size/full speed swing... reduce the size or reduce the speed of your swing until you can produce. Then you can gradually work back up to full size/full speed.

It will take some practice to get used to Smaller or Slower swings but they are valuable tools any time you want to make a change quickly and effectively.

Smaller and Slower both make it easier to raise awareness of specific issues. Full Size and Full Speed make it very difficult for your mind to track your movements accurately.

If someone challenges you to relearn how to write your signature in a different language... do you want to write the entire signature and do it at full speed or would breaking it down and slowing it down be easier?

I recommend you take a few sessions at the range and determine which is the easiest adjustment for you to make accurate swings... some of my students prefer slower and some prefer smaller.

Usually the individual reaction to each option is very polarizing... one method is ok and the other is torture.☺

Take the **"Reduction"** that works best for you and use the **"Opposite Fix"** of *Ball Spotting* to groove *Down the Line* Impact and strike the center of the ball with ideal loft consistently.

The Golf Ball - Review and Goals

Center of the Equator is the Sweet Spot - Contacting anywhere other than the Center of the Equator of the ball drastically reduces your ability to maximize velocity, optimize backspin and minimize sidespin in your shots to the target.

Club Face moving slightly downward with irons at Impact - A slightly downward iron approach gives you the best chance of hitting the equator of the ball and creating optimum Face Loft, distance, spin and trajectory for every shot.

Club Face moving slightly downward or level with hybrids, long irons and fairway woods at Impact - Longer, less lofted clubs will fly further and higher with a very shallow downward approach or even a level approach if the ball is in a good lie or on a tee.

Club Face moving level or slightly upward with driver at Impact - When the ball is on a tee with the driver, a level approach gives you maximum accuracy and a slightly upward approach gives you the potential for optimum distance.

Club Face travelling *Down the Line* at Impact – Training your Club Face to swing toward the target through Impact will help you minimize sidespin, maximize distance and is one of the most efficient uses of your practice time.

These are the basic *Release Zone* approaches your golf ball requires for maximizing Sweet Spot Impact and helping you hit *Sweet Spot Shots* more consistently.

Golf ball design and quality has improved dramatically in the last 20 years. They fly farther and straighter than ever before. When purchasing golf balls, you can even match their construction to your swing characteristics. However, if your swing is not producing contact on the center of the equator of the ball... you will not take advantage of all the amazing technology built into today's golf balls.

The concepts of Sweet Spot ball contact are VERY simple... Down the Line Club Face Path and Correct *Scuff* (Face Loft) are the "Club Face Impact Keys" that all Sweet Spot swings have in common.

The goal is to be able to swing on the golf course without having to think about these keys. Consistently correct repetitions (every day for at least a few weeks) are the only means to adapting your swing to match these patterns. Visualize, make smaller swings, swing slowly... whatever it takes to insure correct practice repetitions and you will begin to trust the new correct movements in your swing and strike the Sweet Spot of the golf ball at impact.

Before reading further and adding more information to your brain... now is a good time to go to the range and make sure you can execute ideal *Down the Line Club Face Path and Correct Club Face Loft/Scuff* on command and with all clubs. If you have begun to experience the benefits of *Down the Line Path* and hitting the Sweet Spot of the golf ball... it is time to explore the Sweet Spot of the Club Face. **You may be surprised to see how much more power and control you can add to your game by wearing out the Sweet Spot on your Club Face.**

CHAPTER 3- THE CLUB FACE

Did you know that if you miss the Sweet Spot of a driver by as little as ½ inch you can lose 20% (or more!) of your distance with the driver?

Did you also know that if your driver Club Face is Aiming as little as 2 degrees away from the target your shots can go 20 yards (or more!) off-line?

New materials, technology and design innovations have made golf clubs much more forgiving. However, shots that are long, straight and to the target will only happen on rare occasions if your Club Face contact is wandering aimlessly toe/heel/high/low on the Club Face or if the Face Aim is more than a few degrees off line.

The height of the Sweet Spot on the Club Face varies slightly from the irons to the hybrids and woods and knowing the difference is critical to your target hitting success.

The fourth Groove up from the bottom is the Sweet Spot for most irons. Not knowing the correct Sweet Spot height on the irons is one of the biggest causes of poor contact that I see on the lesson tee and on the course.

When you hold a golf ball up close to Groove Four of a short iron you will notice that the Club Face must be de-lofted to have the two Sweet Spots connect.

If you add loft... the ball will always strike on the very bottom of the Club Face.

Making sure you have a clear, correct picture of Sweet Spot Impact for the ball and the Club Face does not guarantee great shots... but it does guarantee you will be training movements using an image that will produce great shots. It also means when you do hit good shots... you can take credit for them.

If you are picturing Groove Two as the ideal contact spot... most of your contact will be slightly thin (lots of vibration at impact) and your trajectory will be high and short.

Groove One contact will produce a lot of low flying/gopher seeking missiles and you may also hit the ground before you hit the ball if your club is moving upward before Impact. Contact above Groove Four will produce flight that is too high and short of your target... or the leading edge of the Club Face will hit the ground before it strikes the ball.

Your contact does not have to be perfect. You can produce very effective shots hitting one Groove high or low from ideal.

The "Key" is to start visualizing the center of Groove Four on the irons connecting with the Sweet Spot of the ball. This will help you to produce better quality good shots and begin the process of eliminating a significant number of fat and topped shots.

The center of the Club Face height-wise (from top to bottom), is the Sweet Spot for woods and hybrids.

Contact too high on the Club Face will tend to produce high shots or pop ups. This is often caused by the Club Face approaching on a downward angle that is too steep and the Club Face being de-lofted.

Contact too low on the Club Face will tend to produce low "line drives" or rollers. This is often caused by the Club Face approaching on an upward angle that is to severe and the Club Face having too much Loft at Impact.

Correct Shaft Lean - The Sweet Spots Will Not Meet Without It

If golf clubs had no Loft and the ball was always teed up, you could connect the Sweet Spots with a neutral (vertical) shaft lean.

The challenge is... the ball would not stay in the air very long because the lack of Loft would not produce the backspin necessary to keep the ball flying.

Since all clubs do have Loft and backspin is an important component of every airborne golf shot... it is critical that you train your swing to produce Correct Shaft Lean at Impact on every swing. This will give your Sweet Spot shots the ideal combination of correct spin rate, trajectory and distance.

There are three basic Shaft Lean positions at Impact:

Positive – Hands in front of the ball

Neutral – Hands even with the ball

Negative – Hands behind the ball

Understanding how these Shaft Lean positions affect contact and ball flight will help you create an accurate picture of what your Impact will look like with each of the different clubs in your bag.

Training your swing to execute the correct Shaft Leans for each of the different clubs will guarantee you will no longer give up strokes on the scorecard from topped shots and fat shots.

Positive Shaft Lean

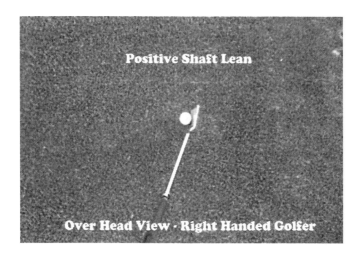

Positive Shaft Lean at Impact... is when your hands (at the top of the club) are closer to the target than the Club Face is. This produces a slightly downward "trapping" angle of approach of the Club Face to the ball and a de-lofted Club Face. **Positive Shaft Lean and a slightly downward angle of approach are the ideal *Release Zone* movements for most iron shots.**

Sweet Spot Helpful Hint

If you want to train ideal Positive Shaft Lean... train your Guiding Hand to swing to the middle of your left thigh at Impact with every swing for every club.

When your Guiding Hand is opposite your left thigh at Impact (for right handed golfers) ... you can make slight adjustments to ball position and get ideal Shaft Lean without having to change the feel of your swing motion.

Touring professionals average roughly 2 clubs (6-8 degrees) of Positive Shaft Lean when they strike the ball with all irons up to the 5 iron.

This would give an 8 iron the loft of a 6 iron at Impact... optimizing Sweet Spot contact, backspin AND increasing distance.

If you do not get enough Positive Shaft Lean, striking Groove Four of the irons with the ball resting on the ground becomes extremely difficult... especially with high-lofted irons when the ball is sitting on short grass or firm turf.

Positive Shaft Lean (decreased Loft) is one of the few things in golf that can give you more control AND more distance.

The increase in distance comes from the decrease in Loft and increased compression of the ball at Impact.

The greater control is a result of increased back spin due to the slightly downward movement of the Club Face and the trapping of the ball between the Club Face and the ground.

Sweet Spot Shaft Lean/Loft Tip -

The golf clubs are designed to produce the correct amount of Loft/altitude for your shots.

There is no need for you to add more Loft to the Club Face at Impact, it will just create incorrect Shaft Lean and cause poor contact.

Your job is to move the ball "forward" to the target... let the Club Face design take care of the "up".

Neutral Shaft Lean

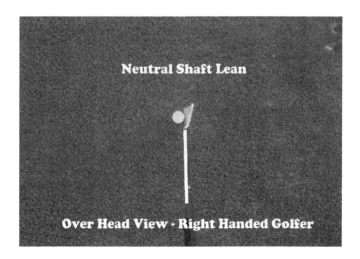

Your hands are the same distance from the target as the Club Face is at Impact (the shaft is perpendicular to the ground). The Neutral Shaft Lean produces a level "sweeping" *Release Zone* movement and a Neutral Loft of the Club Face. Neutral Lean with hybrids and shallow faced fairway woods can produce higher launching shots that land softly. A level sweep can also work with long irons if the grass is not too short or the turf too firm.

The only time a Neutral Lean can produce Groove Four contact with short irons is if the ball is teed up or sitting high in light rough or long fairway grass. If your goal is optimum spin rate for stopping power and trajectory control, a Neutral Lean is the second-best option in most cases... especially with the mid and short irons. A level sweep (Neutral Lean) does produce more Loft but does not create the spin that will make shots stop on the green or the compression that makes them fly further.

Negative Shaft Lean

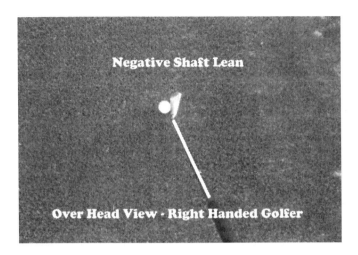

Your hands are farther from the target than the Club Face is at Impact... and the Club Face has too much Loft. This is the shaft angle with irons, hybrids and fairway woods that causes most fat and topped shots.

If you attempt to scoop, lift or get underneath the ball and help it up into the air with your swing... you will create Negative Shaft Lean at Impact.

Even if you make decent contact, Negative Shaft Lean will produce excessively high, short shots with the short irons and low trajectory, low spin, short flying shots with the long clubs. The **only** time a slight Negative Shaft Lean can potentially help your shots is with the driver.

If you tee the ball high and swing slightly upward (3 or 4 degrees) this can help you create a higher launch angle and low spin... both of which can add distance to your drives.

Sweet Spot Simple Tip -

How much Positive Shaft Lean should you be striving for? Simple... when the ball is resting on the ground lean your shaft forward until the Groove Four of the irons (center of the Club Face with hybrids and fairway woods) meets the equator of the ball.

You will notice significantly more Positive Shaft Lean is necessary with the higher lofted clubs to achieve optimum Sweet Spot contact. You can achieve the desired Shaft Lean by changing ball position (moving the ball back in the stance) or by changing hand position (moving the hands further forward in the stance). Changing hand position will create less swing compensation issues and less directional issues than changing ball position. When you move the ball back in your stance (away from the target), it should be easy to get your hands out front... but the ball will tend to get pushed to the right and curve back to the left. **The easiest way to achieve Positive Shaft Lean with your swing is to set the Shaft Lean you desire at address and practice returning to the same position at Impact ("Snapshot" practice... swinging the Guiding Hand to the middle of the left thigh at Impact is a great method to help retrain your Impact image).**

Grooving Positive Shaft Lean

Slow Motion/Snapshots

Correct shaft angle at Impact is VERY difficult to monitor when you are swinging at full speed.

One of the keys to Effective change is making sure you can tell the difference between correct and incorrect repetitions EVERY swing.

Every incorrect swing you make can hold back your improvement process.

Swinging slower and pausing in a correct *Release Zone* impact position ("Snapshot" practice) guarantees a higher percentage of correct repetitions which leads to faster, easier pattern change.

Swinging at 25% to 50% of normal speed dramatically heightens accurate *feel* of swing movements... and pausing in the correct Impact Shaft Lean position ("Snapshot") creates a strong visual image of the goal.

Watch yourself in a mirror while you perform repetitions and add in some "eyes closed" repetitions... to dramatically speed the learning curve for being able to *see* and *feel* correct Shaft Lean.

Once you are confident that you can repeat correct shaft lean performing Slow Motion/Stop Action swings, begin making full size slow motion swings.

Add speed and a golf ball only when you know you are executing quality repetitions.

The Club Face - Review and Goals

CENTER of the Club Face (toe to heel) is the Sweet Spot with all clubs - When the ball contact is more on the toe this will often cause the toe to slow down creating an open Club Face and sending the ball to the right (when the path is Down the Line or Back to the Inside). When the ball contact is on the heel, the opposite occurs (unless the path is too much From the Inside... which can create the dreaded shank). More than a quarter of an inch to either side can have a dramatic effect on your ability to hit targets. Slightly heel side contact with irons has less negative effects than toe side contact. The opposite is true for the driver.

Groove Four is Sweet Spot height for irons - If you want to create optimum distance control with your irons, contact at the correct height on the Club Face is crucial. If the contact is low, the ball will fly lower and will not stop if it lands on the green. If the contact is too high on the face, the ball may fly higher and shorter... or the turf may fly further than the ball. The contact does not have to be perfect but, one groove either side of ideal is the margin for error you have... if you desire precise distance control.

CENTER of the Club Face (height-wise) is the Sweet Spot height for hybrids and woods - Tremendous design improvements have made hybrids and woods more forgiving than the irons with respect to correct contact height. **But, if you want to achieve consistent trajectory and distance control, practice finding the right height on the Club Face with all your clubs.**

Positive Shaft Lean is Optimum for all clubs except driver - Because of the Loft on the irons (especially the short irons), finding the Sweet Spot can only happen on a consistent basis when you lean the club shaft forward at Impact. This translates to getting your hands closer to the target than the ball is at Impact.

Neutral Shaft Lean is Optimum for driver and can also works with long irons, hybrids and fairway woods - Clubs with very little loft (4 iron or longer if your Club Face speed is less than 100 mph with a driver) work most efficiently when they are contacted with a Neutral Shaft Lean. This will create a sweeping motion in the *Release Zone* which promotes the correct launch angle and ideal trajectory to reach more par fives and make par fours play shorter.

ALL Effective Sweet Spot Swings create Correct Shaft Lean.

Connect the Sweet Spots and Lean the Shaft correctly as the Club Face is moving *Down the Line* in the *Release Zone* and you will be amazed at the look and feel of your golf shots. Short irons will fly lower, longer and stop quicker on the green. Long irons and hybrids will fly higher and carry further. Drivers will carry further, have a flatter trajectory and roll more when they land to get you closer to every green.

Correct Shaft Lean is one of the most powerful tools at your disposal if you desire solid contact and maximum distance control from every shot.

Shaft Lean can be a challenge to change. Hitting balls at the range is the least effective way to make this change.

When hitting balls during the change process... your body wants to do what it has always done and your mind wants to create the new pattern.

Winning this battle between body and brain is the key to successful change.

Making tough changes by doing the same thing your body has always done (hitting balls at the range) is not going to help your mind win the battle and execute permanent change.

Be smart with your Shaft Lean practice.

Do lots of super slow motion swings in front of a mirror and swings without any golf ball BEFORE you start hitting balls at the driving range.

In many ways, it is like learning to write your signature. Start slowly and make sure you are executing the letters correctly before signing an important check at full speed.

Are you ready to get the complete picture of THE part of your *swing* that has the most Direct Influence on your *Club Face Keys at Impact*?

Then it is time for you to learn about the *Release Zone*.

CHAPTER 4- THE RELEASE ZONE

You now know where the Sweet Spot on the ball is

You know where the Sweet Spot on the Club Face is...

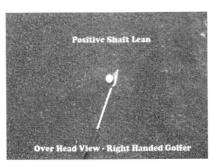

You know Positive Lean Connects the Sweet Spots...

Now it is time to get a clear picture of the part of *your* swing that Directly Influences these goals and creates ideal movement of the Club Face at Impact.

It is called the *Release Zone.* *The Release Zone is the part of your swing where you translate the Club Face Impact Keys into a repeatable full swing motion you can trust on the golf course.*

The Release Zone

Training your Club Face to move efficiently in the downswing *Release Zone* achieves the most dramatic results with the least amount of changes to your swing. Tour pros have unusual takeaways, top of the backswings and transitions and even finishes... so can you. Tour pros Club Face movements in the *Release Zone* are remarkably similar... I want to help you improve yours.

Why do I call it the *Release Zone*?

Because, during *Effective* Sweet Spot swings (with correct Club Face Impact Keys) the Club Face is *"released to the target"* as opposed to... attempting to *"hit the ball"*. This *release* is felt in the Guiding Hand (and the right wrist and elbow). It feels like you are *throwing/releasing* the club shaft and the Club Face "to the target".

Sweet Spot Simple Tip

Throwing a club (preferably an old one you do not care about... in an area where no one can get hurt!) is a great way for developing an accurate feel for releasing the club "to the target".

When you do this exercise correctly, the club will fly directly to your target on a low trajectory. When you are hitting shots to targets... your golf swing should feel like you are throwing the club to the target. If you do not release it... it will never go to the target.

Inefficient swings attempt to "hit the ball" from the top of the backswing... instead of *releasing/throwing* the Club Face to the target... in the *Release Zone*. A "hit the ball" mindset promotes excess tension, uses too much force and is a very difficult motion to repeat consistently.

Imagine the difference between "hitting" something with your fist... and throwing a ball. When hitting, your hand is clenched tight and you would use all your muscle to deliver the blow. When throwing, your hand is relaxed and you use momentum to create speed. Force versus speed... hit versus swing/ throw.

Swinging the golf club and then *releasing* it to the target in the Release Zone... encourages rhythm without tension, *Speed* without force and makes consistency much more achievable.

Imagine a pendulum. If the pendulum is aimed correctly and swung from the same center, repeating the motion is easily achievable with minimum physical AND mental effort.

Optimum *Release Zone* movement is the foundation for an *Effective* Sweet Spot swing that produces *Sweet Spot Shots* on a consistent basis.

The takeaway, the top of back swing and the and the finish of your swing have no precise right or wrong... only what works best for you.

Your personal grip, setup and swing movements should all be designed to make it as easy as possible for you to repeat Optimum *Release Zone* movement.

The Release Zone Big Four – The Building Blocks for YOUR Effective Swing

1. Late Club Face *Rotation*
2. Timed Club Face *Speed*
3. Optimum Club Face Path
4. Optimum Club Face Loft

<u>**Release Zone Building Block #1**</u>

Late Club Face Rotation

Many golfers who come to me for help… assume that squaring the Club Face early and keeping it square as long as possible, will help them control the direction of their shots.

This can be valid for putting and chipping but, in the full swing this will most often cause short and crooked shots.

If you square the Club Face early in the Release Zone… you will be forced to hold the Club Face square until Impact in order to hit a straight shot. This holding the Club Face square slows the Club Face down and creates tension in your hands and arms.

Also, once the Club Face squares to the target… it's momentum starts moving left of the target line and upward. Neither of which helps you hit quality shots to your target.

A late, quick squaring/*rotation* of the Club Face adds velocity, improves Shaft Lean and helps minimize hooks and slices.

79

It may surprise you to hear that tour pros have been measured with as much as 19 mph more rotational speed of the toe of the Club Face than the heel of the Club Face... at Impact.

This means they are "letting" the Club Face *rotate* (*release*) very quickly in the *Release Zone.*

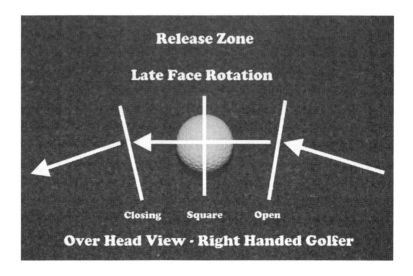

Attempting to "hold" the Club Face square too long in the *Release Zone* is the one of the most common causes of Path moving *Back to the Inside* too soon, lack of distance and injuries to the wrists and elbows.

Also... the draw flight many golfers prefer is most efficiently produced when the Club Face is fractionally open at Impact, the path is slightly *From the Inside* and the face releases/rotates fully after Impact. This Impact Dynamic produces a flight that starts right of the target and finishes curving back to the target (for right handed golfers).

Here are a few of the advantages of Late Club Face Rotation:

- **It helps to correctly time the *Speed* of the Club Face in the swing.**

  One of the big influences on *Club Face Speed* is when the toe rotates past the heel in the swing. Squaring the Club Face early usually means the Club Face will reach *Maximum Speed* before Impact and then decelerate through Impact.

  This causes distance AND contact issues because your Club Face is slowing down as it strikes the ball and can also hit the ground before it strikes the ball.

- **It helps create Positive Shaft Lean at Impact.**

  The further your arms swing toward the target before squaring the Club Face, the further your hands will be ahead of the ball at Impact and the more Positive Shaft lean you create.

  Many tour pros *square/rotate* the Club Face so late they have Positive Shaft Lean even with the driver.

- **It helps keep the club in the correct Down the Line Path at impact**.

   Once the Club Face squares to the target it begins to move *Back to the Inside.*

   Squaring the Club Face too early thus makes it very difficult to keep the Club Face travelling Down the Line at Impact and can also inhibit a full *rotation/release* of the Club Face.

- **It helps minimize sidespin**.

   Since *squaring* the Club Face early causes the path of the Club Face to move *Back to the Inside* too early... it also contributes to excess sidespin.

   The more the Club Face is moving away from the target at Impact... the more sidespin you create at the end of the flight.

Late is Great... when it comes to squaring your Club Face.

Grooving Late Face Rotation

Small Swings

In a full-size swing, controlling Club Face *rotation* consistently can be difficult for players of all levels. This is one of the reasons why even the tour pros average hitting only 65% of the fairways and 70% of the greens in regulation.

As with all changes, it is critical to make sure you can accurately assess the timing of your Club Face *rotation* each swing. Start by making swings where the Club Face stops at waist high on the backswing and the follow through.

Since the goal is to improve your swing in the Release Zone... why not practice any new movement just in the Release Zone? This dramatically improves accuracy and awareness during the learning process.

In the backswing when the Club Face is waist high... the toe of the Club Face should be pointing straight up. A slightly closed position can also be *Effective* here... if you have a strong body *rotation* through Impact to minimize closed Club Face Impacts.

The palm of your Guiding hand and the back of your upper hand should be roughly parallel to the target line at this point.

As you swing toward the target, keep the Club Face open relative to the target (toe pointing upward) by not forcing/allowing your hands to rotate until they are in front of your trailing leg thigh (hands directly under the trailing shoulder). **There is no need to use force in your hands to keep the Club Face open. If you do not "actively" *rotate* your hands or forearms... the Club Face will stay open on its own.**

Sweet Spot Helpful Hint –

It may take some very attentive practice repetitions before you can feel if your hands are "actively" rotating the Club Face early. Clearly identifying whether your hands/forearms are "actively" rotating the Club Face is a very important step in translating knowledge of the Club Face Impact Keys into a Sweet Spot swing.

Ideally... the *rotation* should be more of a *releasing*/letting go/passive move than a hitting/forcing/active move.

Let the momentum of the swing and the weight of the Club Head *rotate* the Club Face for you. Try some small, slow swings and just let the Club Head swing. You should be able to feel the Club Face *rotating* on its own. If you can't... you may be gripping too tightly or you may need to do several swings with your eyes closed to be able to feel it accurately.

Rotating your "core/torso" through Impact as you allow your Guiding Hand to rotate... can also help make sure the Club Face *squares* at Impact and *releases* fully after Impact.

By the time the Club Face reaches waist high in the follow through the toe of the club should be pointed to the sky again.

This is also the end of the *Release Zone*.

The hands and Club Face are waist high in the follow through and the leading edge of the Club Face is perpendicular to the ground... square.

The amount of hip/core *rotation* may vary at this point from golfer to golfer. Your chest should be almost facing the target and your weight should be almost fully transferred to your left side at this point. **It is also helpful to have your arms fully extended and your hands "letting" the club "fly" to the target.**

The palm of your lower hand (Guiding Hand) and the back of your upper hand should have also returned to parallel to the target line.

The goal is to get comfortable with the feel of your Club Face and hands *rotating* 180 degrees from the downswing *Release Point* to waist high in the follow through (end of the *Release Zone*).

Use whatever club or swing speed that makes it easiest for you to get positive results as quickly as possible.

When you feel comfortable that you can make "waist high" small/half swings and execute them correctly on a consistent basis... you can move on to "shoulder high" medium/three quarter swings.

Take your time working up to full swings.

This late, quick *rotation/release* of the Club Face is one of the easiest ways to create more distance in your shots with every club in the bag.

The movement should feel like the *release* in your hand and wrist when you throw a ball.

The most powerful and repeatable golf swings are throws... not hits.

It is critical to remember to keep your hands and arms relaxed and LET the Club Face turn late and quickly.

Do not try to use tension to hold the Club Face open and then force it to rotate closed.

Extra tension in the grip can cause slices and thin or topped shots and means you must consciously "time" the release as opposed to letting the club design and swing dynamics do the work for you.

Release Zone Building Block #2

Club Face Speed Timing

One of THE fastest and most *Effective* ways to create a repeating swing... is to correctly time when the Club Face reaches *Maximum Speed*.

Ideally the Club Face should reach *Maximum Speed* just AFTER impact.

This means the Club Face will be **accelerating** when it strikes the ball.

Here is an example of how important timing the Club Face *Maximum Speed* is:

Picture two different swings striking a ball with Sweet Spot contact at 100 mph.

Swing #1 – the Club Face is moving 90 mph before Impact and 110 mph after impact... *accelerating* at Impact.

Swing #2 – the Club Face is moving 110mph before Impact and 90mph after Impact... decelerating at Impact.

Swing #1 will produce a shot that can travel 10% farther (or more).

Why?

Because the Impact Dynamics that produce an *accelerating* Club Face create more Smash Factor (a calculation of ball speed relative to Club Face Speed) than a decelerating Club Face.

The main reason for this is the quality of the strike on the Club Face and the compression, trajectory and spin it creates (shaft unload also has an affect).

Wouldn't you like 10% more distance just by correctly timing the *Club Face Speed* you already have?

Speed Timing also has a powerful effect on Shaft Lean. Once the Club Face reaches *Maximum Speed* it is at full extension. From full extension, the Club Face begins to travel upward and the shaft begins to move toward a Negative Lean position. Later *acceleration* means more Positive Lean at Impact.

The main cause of poor *Speed* Timing of the Club Face is an incorrect "mental image", which causes poor swing sequence at the start of the downswing... also called "casting" or "hitting from the top".

Most golfers try to *accelerate* the Club Face as quickly as possible from the top of the backswing "to the ball". Tour pros *accelerate* the Club Face smoothly from the start of the *Release Zone* "to the target".

The Club Face can only reach Maximum Speed once in the swing. If you do it early as a result of accelerating "to the ball"... your Club Face will be slowing down at Impact.

Take a minute and make sure you understand the difference between these two concepts and how they relate to Speed:

To the Ball vs. To the Target.

Sweet Spot Simple Tip

If you want to hit more targets... accelerate your Club Face "to the target" every swing.

Accelerating **"to the ball" causes:**

A hurried transition from backswing to downswing

A steep downswing and a path that moves *Back to the Inside* to soon

Club Face outpacing the arms and body (casting)

Full Speed and full extension before Impact

Accelerating **"to the target" creates:**

A smooth unhurried transition

A shallower downswing and *Down the Line Path* at Impact

Arms and body leading the Club Face (lag)

Full Speed and full extension after Impact... towards the target

If you desire a repeating swing from club to club and shot to shot... you MUST learn to time your *Club Face Speed* correctly on a consistent basis.

Grooving *Club Face Speed* Timing

The Whoosh

The simplest way to begin to train correct *Club Face Speed*... is to use your ears.

When you swing the Club Face it makes a **Whoosh** sound.

The faster the Club Face is moving, the louder the sound is.

If your **Whoosh** is very quiet, try holding your club near the face of the club and swinging the handle (turn the club upside down). Since the handle is lighter than the Club Face... you will be able to get more **Speed** and it will make more noise.

The key is not the volume of the *Whoosh*... it is the timing of the *Whoosh*.

The loudest part of the *Whoosh* happens when the Club Face is going the fastest (*Maximum Speed*).

When you first begin practicing the **Whoosh** drill you may need to close your eyes while swinging to be able to accurately hear **exactly** where the **Whoosh** is loudest.

Ideally... the loudest part of the *Whoosh* should be immediately after Impact for every swing with every club.

It is the rolling over of your forearms (*releasing/rotating* the toe of the Club Face) and the unhinging of your wrists and right elbow (*releasing the Club Shaft*) that create the *Whoosh* in your swing.

This drill must be done without a ball until you can feel a rhythm to your swing that helps the **Whoosh** to happen naturally/easily in the correct place.

It is also VERY important to practice this drill with different clubs to get used to the feel of different length shafts *Whooshing* in the correct place.

Sweet Spot Bonus - Correcting your *Whoosh* timing... will also improve your *Scuff!*

Release Zone Building Block #3

Optimum Club Face Path

At a PGA Tournament, I used a swing analyzer and studied the Impact Club Face Key dynamics of more than 1000 tournament spectators during the week-long event.

Over 80% of Touring Professionals swing on a Club Face Path between 0 degrees (directly *Down the Line*) and 3 degrees *From the Inside.*

Only 2 tournament spectators out of the over 1000 that I analyzed... swung in the same Club Face Path as the Touring Professionals. *Only 2 out of more than 1000.*

When your Path is more than 5 degrees away from *Down the Line*... you start creating excess sidespin that means hitting *Sweet Spot Shots* to your targets becomes more accidental than intentional.

Most of the spectators were 5-15 degrees *Back to the Inside* (travelling left) at Impact and some were more than 45 degrees *Back to the Inside.*

Imagine how challenging it must be to hit your target... when the Club Face is travelling in a Path up to 45 degrees away from your target.

Even if your Club Face was Aiming *Down the Line* at Impact... your ball would still spin 20 yards or more to the right of your intended target with a driver.

Remember... the amount of sidespin at the end of your shots is strongly influenced by the Path your Club Face is travelling on at Impact. The further your Path is away from ideal... the bigger your slices and hooks.

Not to mention how difficult it is to hit the center of the equator of the ball with the center of the Club Face... if the Club Face is moving across the ball instead of into the back center of the ball.

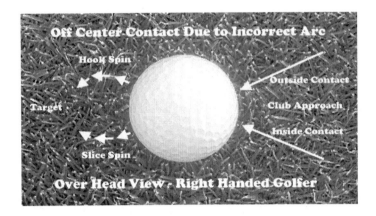

You should not try to emulate *everything* that tour pros execute in their swings.

But, if you do want your golf ball to fly powerfully to the target with solid contact and minimal sidespin... matching the *Down the Line Path* of the tour pros in the *Release Zone* is a great goal for your swing.

Your Path does not have to be perfect. But, the closer to *Down the Line* your Path is... the better your good shots will be and the less your bad shots will penalize you.

Grooving Down the Line Club Face Path

Goalposts

Place a ball on the ground. Place two long driver tees in the ground like a pair of goalposts. One tee will be outside the target line and one inside the target line. The tees should be placed slightly wider than your Club Face... depending on how much you want to challenge yourself. To achieve maximum feedback, place another tee four inches before Impact in line with the outside tee and another tee four inches after Impact in line with the inside tee.

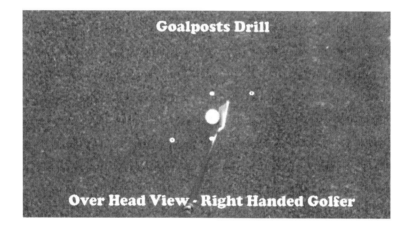

The goal is simple. Hit shots without your Club Face hitting the goalposts. If your Club Face Path is correct you should be able to hit shots without touching the goal posts. This drill is effective with all clubs but, especially with the driver since the effects of Club Face Path are magnified most with the longest clubs with the least amount of loft. Correct Club Face Path with the driver will help you maximize your good shots and minimize the effect of the less than ideal swings.

Release Zone Building Block #4

Optimum Club Face Loft

Solid Sweet Spot contact is the fastest route to distance and trajectory control.

When you contact the correct groove on the Club Face your shots will have consistent backspin rates. This is the only way to know how high and how far each of your shots will fly with a specific club.

Every time you hit a shot there is a distance "window" of where your ball could end up.

The closer you are to optimum Club Face Loft/Shaft Lean at Impact, the smaller the distance "window" of where your shots will end up.

This will allow you to pick accurate distance targets AND the correct clubs for each of your shots on the golf course. Solid contact and distance control is also one of the quickest ways to hit more greens with your approach shots and lower your scores.

Sweet Spot Performance Question -

How many yards away from the green can you be... and hit the green more than 75% of the time?

For the average golfer that shoots 100... 30 yards is the 75% accuracy distance. Groove your Club Face Loft with your wedges and 100 yards is an achievable goal. How many shots would this save you every round?

Anytime the ball is on the ground, de-lofting the Club Face/creating Positive Shaft Lean is THE critical element in repeating Sweet Spot contact, controlling your distance and hitting more *Sweet Spot Shots*.

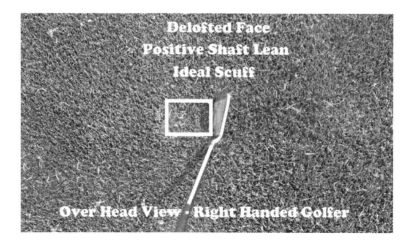

The longer and lower lofted the club, the less de-lofting/Positive Shaft Lean you need to create but, you should strive for a "hands in front/de-lofted" Impact position for all shots when the ball is resting on the ground.

Optimum Club Face Loft/Shaft Lean is a powerful component of your ability to control distance, control trajectory, generate power and hit more targets.

With your short irons (8 iron down through the wedges), aggressive Positive Shaft Lean:

- **Adds spin to help your shots stop on the green**
- **Maximizes solid contact at Impact**

With your mid irons (7 iron up through the 5 iron), moderate Positive Shaft Lean:

- **Adds spin for direction and distance control**
- **Creates higher trajectory from optimum launch**

With long irons, hybrids and fairway woods minimal Positive Shaft Lean:

- **Maximizes carry distance**
- **Minimizes poor contact**

Grooving Correct Club Face Loft/Shaft Lean

The Lag Drill

If you want to create ideal Club Face Loft/Shaft Lean, then you need to create a *Lag* time between when your hands reach the golf ball and when your Club Face reaches the golf ball... in your downswing.

Imagine starting a stopwatch when your hands get to the golf ball... and stopping it when the Club Face reaches the golf ball. The longer the time gap, the greater the *Lag*/Shaft Lean you are creating.

"Snapshot" rehearsals can be very helpful *Lag* training at first.

I recommend combining this with the *Scuff* drill to get even more feedback about your *Lag* and Shaft Lean.

Ideally the *Scuff* should always start in the middle of your stance... meaning you have created Positive Shaft Lean and correct *Lag*.

If your *Scuff* is starting more than an inch before the center of your stance (further from the target) you are creating Negative Shaft Lean at Impact and the Club Face is reaching the ball before your hands (Negative *Lag* time/Negative Shaft Lean).

If your *Scuff* is starting more than two inches past the center of your stance (closer to the target), you are creating too much Positive Shaft Lean (this is quite rare). If this does happen it is usually caused by your body sliding or shifting to the left... as opposed to creating too much *Lag*.

The shorter the club... the longer the *Scuff* will be and the shorter the *Lag* time will be. The longer the club... the shorter the *Scuff* will be and the longer the *Lag* time.

With a Driver, there will be no *Scuff* and you will have the longest *Lag* time. This one of the reasons so many people struggle with the driver. When we try to move the Club Face to the ball too soon... we lose all our *Lag* time and the Club Face gets in positions that can require GPS to locate our drives.

Good things come to golfers who wait... for the Club Face to catch up to the hands in the *Release Zone*.

Sweet Spot Helpful Hint

Here is a helpful hint when it comes to grooving optimum *Release Zone* movements for your swing:

Even though there are 4 keys to optimum *Release Zone* movement and each is very important...

Grooving Late Club Face Rotation and Correct Club Face Speed Timing are a great Minimum Change/Maximum Result formula for helping you master Club Face Path and Club Face Loft as well.

Spent a few minutes every day for a couple weeks swinging the club focusing only on the *feel* of when the toe of the Club Face rotates past the heel and when the "***Whoosh***" is the loudest... and you will notice big improvements in *Club Face Path* and *Club Face Loft* as well. A four for two swing training bonus!

Start this process with no golf ball. No golf ball makes it much easier for you to retrain your swing patterns.

As soon as you place a ball in front of you... your body wants to execute the same swing pattern it has always executed. Imagine changing your posture... it would take a lot of focused repetitions before the new posture becomes comfortable enough for you to have it happen without you thinking about it.

The same is true for your golf swing. Set yourself a goal that you will do whatever it takes to make sure you always have 80% successful repetitions... and you will improve much faster and retain the improvements longer.

The Release Zone - Review and Goals

Let the Club Face square late - Late Club Face *Rotation* creates optimum power and consistency with the least amount of effort. If you imagine the difference between throwing a ball with no wrist snap and throwing a ball with a late, quick release of the wrist you will get an accurate picture of how much positive effect a late Club Face *Release* can have on your golf shots.

***Release* the Club Face fully after squaring** - Full *Rotation* of the Club Face after Impact minimizes the chance of slices AND the wear and tear on your body during the swing. Holding on and trying to control the R*otation* of the Club Face puts tremendous strain on wrists, elbows and the neck and back. If you want to eliminate slices and keep your body healthy for years of great golf, FULLY *Releasing* the Club Face is a great goal.

Accelerate *through* Impact TO THE TARGET - Groove a rhythm to your swing that dials in the timing of the Club Face acceleration to reach *Full Speed* just after Impact with every club. Poor contact will disappear and your shots will fly farther with less effort than you ever thought possible. **This is one of the most powerful and influential pieces of your Sweet Spot swing.**

Contact the ball in the *Down the Line* part of the Path with every club - If you want the ball to fly to the target, release your Club Face *Down the Line* to the target at Impact. This seems to be one of the most intuitive Essential Elements/Club Face Impact Keys, yet the reality is that very few golfers accomplish this goal.

Down the Line Path **can be accomplished in any number of ways but...**

ALL Sweet Spot swings repeat the *Down the Line* Path... in the correct part of the *Release Zone*.

De-loft the Club Face/Positive Lean the shaft with every club except the driver - The more lofted the club, the more you need to "de-loft/Positive Lean" it to meet the Sweet Spot of the ball with the Sweet Spot of the club.

Let your *Scuffs*/divots be your coach - If they start in the middle of your stance with the toe and heel equal depth and travel towards your target, you will barely feel the ball contacting the Club Face as it rockets off toward your target.

Now you have an accurate picture of what creates a Sweet Spot swing in the *Release Zone* and how that relates to correct Club Face Impact Keys.

This is THE most important part of *your* Sweet Spot golf swing.

Takeaways, transitions and finishes can be unique but, the Club Face movements in the *Release Zone* of Sweet Spot golfers are remarkably similar.

It is time to learn my Evolutionary method for grooving ideal *Release Zone* movement. Turn the page to experience the ease and simplicity of Guiding Hand swing training.

CHAPTER 5- THE GUIDING HAND
TRAIN IT... SO YOU CAN TRUST IT

The amount of information available in golf instruction today can make learning a swing that produces *Sweet Spot Shots* incredibly complex, confusing and frustrating.

Reducing the complexities of the swing to simple Essential concepts that any golfer can master is the Core Philosophy of my teaching.

Simplicity can only be achieved when you focus on the moving parts that have the most **"Direct Influence"** on the quality of your golf shots.

The Club Face movement in the *Release Zone* is the only "Direct Influence" on the golf ball.

Your Guiding Hand is the most "Direct Influence" on the Club Face.

The Guiding Hand is the lower hand on the grip and the closest part of your body to the Club Face. It is also one of the most sensitive and dexterous parts of your body... which will help you raise awareness of correct versus incorrect movements of your Club Face. FYI... I am left handed and Guiding Hand training works great when I make changes to my swing.

Once you have raised the accuracy of your awareness you can maintain control in the Guiding Hand or transfer it to another part of the body.

No other body part mirrors the movement of the Club Face or has as much influence "Guiding" ideal Club Face movement in the *Release Zone*.

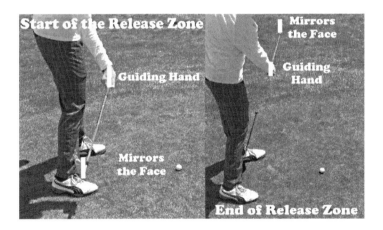

When you hold the club in the correct position with the correct pressure... the Guiding Hand movement mirrors the movement of the Club Face. Why do I call it the Guiding Hand? Because *guiding* the club implies less effort/less control and is more effective than "hitting" at the ball. It also implies "letting" the club rhythmically swing instead of "forcing" it to abruptly hit the ball.

Sweet Spot Clarification

The most common questions/comments I receive from students and readers regarding the Guiding Hand are:

Isn't it difficult to "time" the late Club Face squaring correctly and consistently?

The answer is...

If you "guide" the Club Face correctly in the backswing and at the start of the downswing, the momentum of the swing and the design of the club WILL produce optimum Release Zone timing for you.

Restricting or minimizing Club Face rotation is just as difficult as Releasing and must also be timed correctly... so why not allow the club and your body to give you more distance and more consistent timing with less work?

If you would like to view video lessons explaining in detail how the pros execute late Club Face Rotation and how you can easily do it too... check out the **Sweet Spot Shots Video Series** *on Amazon Video Direct.*

In the learning process... the key is to raise your awareness of what the correct *Guiding* and *Releasing* feels like and looks like.

Swinging with your eyes closed and swinging in front of a mirror will help you build feel and visual trust that your swing is moving correctly.

When performing/playing... the trust you have built in practice will allow you stop thinking about the swing (*the process*) and focus on the target (*the goal*).

Optimum performance always happens when your focus is on the goal... not the process.   Imagine focusing on the movement of your feet and knees when driving your car in city traffic.

Guide and *Release* the Club Face with your Guiding Hand during focused practice sessions... and you will begin to build trust that your swing will become more consistent, more powerful, require less effort and less thought on the course.

The Club Face controls ball flight

The Guiding Hand directs the Club Face

Correct Guiding Hand movements translate DIRECTLY into Effective *Release Zone* Club Face movement, more *Sweet Spot Shots* and more targets hit.

For most golfers, the Guiding Hand is also the most dexterous part of the body and the easiest to train when seeking to establish new patterns.

You spend your life writing, eating and throwing with the Guiding Hand. Why not use this familiar and powerful tool to simplify the learning process and dramatically increase your awareness of *correct* versus *incorrect* movements in your swing?

Remember, once you have used the Guiding Hand to train your *Club Face Impact Keys*... you may or may not find the Guiding Hand is not your best focus "cue" for on-course performance.

I have a lot of students who continue to use the Guiding Hand as their performance "cue". But many of my students do find it more effective to move their focus to a larger and less prone to nerves body part... for more *effective* on-course performance.

My suggestions for areas of the body to test in your practice sessions would be:

- **Shoulders**
- **Chest**
- **Core**

They are easy to monitor and have all worked well for a variety of students.

The Guiding Hand Basics

Let's start with making sure you are holding the club in a way that will make correct Guiding Hand movements as easy as possible.

There are two very important basic elements to connecting your Guiding Hand to the club effectively.

Connecting Your Guiding Hand to the Club Face

1. **Position - make squaring simpler**
2. **Pressure - make timing simpler**

Not all golfers will hold the club with the same position and the same pressure.

However, following the basic guidelines in the next few pages will make a big difference in how easy it is for your Club Face to square correctly, for you to time the *Release* correctly and to tune your swing to hit more *Sweet Spot Shots*.

Remember... Club Face Aim at Impact is the strongest "Direct Influence" on the direction of your golf shots. 2 Degrees away from square at Impact is enough for you to miss the fairway with your driver.

Getting the position of your Guiding Hand correct on the club is a great way to make correct Club Face Aim at Impact much easier for your body to repeat... without your brain having to control it.

Guiding Hand Basic Element #1

Position of the Guiding Hand

Matching the position of the palm of your Guiding Hand to the leading edge of the Club Face is the easiest way to help your Guiding Hand square the Club Face without conscious control.

The leading edge (bottom edge for irons and top edge for hybrids and woods) of the Club Face should always be set 90 degrees (square) to the target line at address with the intent of returning there at Impact. The palm of the Guiding Hand should mirror this position. **Imagine a laser beam facing the same direction as the palm of your Guiding Hand. It should point directly to the target (or slightly to the right of the target.**

When the Guiding Hand palm matches the leading edge of the Club Face, you will have a clear, simple visual of what you need to do to return the Club Face to square at Impact.

For most golfers' this is also the natural hanging position of the palm from the shoulder (Try it!).

This means the natural movement pattern of your body is going to help you get the Club Face back to square at Impact.

Also, full Club Face *rotation* after Impact will require as little effort and training as possible for this critical aspect of *Release Zone* movement.

Sweet Spot Helpful Hint

Aiming your Guiding Hand (right) palm slightly to the right of the target (when addressing the ball) can also work very well.

Especially if you have had issues with leaving the Club Face open at Impact. I would not recommend aiming your right palm to the left of the target... it will cause a lot of pulls and slices.

Holding the club mostly in the fingers of the Guiding Hand makes it easier to let the Club Face *rotate* quickly to promote *Club Face Speed* and minimize Face Aim that is too open at Impact.

As you can see in the next picture, the club grip runs from the middle knuckle of the index finger to the natural crease between the fingers and the palm at the top end of the grip.

What about the Left Hand (non-Guiding Hand)?

If you look two pictures ahead, you will see "two knuckles" of my left hand in view. This is considered a neutral grip and helps both hands work well together. "Three knuckles" on the left hand is a "stronger" grip and helps *rotation* at impact. Experiment to find which works best for you. I would caution against a "one knuckle" grip (weak) and a four "knuckle grip" (very strong) because they require extra compensations in the rest of the body to consistently square the Club Face.

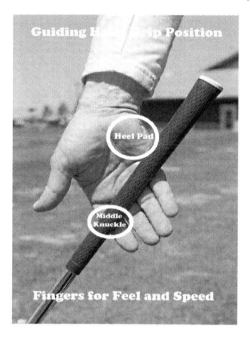

Keeping the grip under the heel pad and in the fingers also helps you maintain control of the club without having to use excessive force.

We know from the *Release Zone* Big Four that the goal is to let the Club Face *rotate* as late, as quickly and fully as possible.

The muscles in the fingers are small, fast twitch fibers and some of the quickest muscles in the body. Holding the club in the fingers of the Guiding Hand makes a late, quick *Rotation* much easier than if the club is held in the palm.

Holding the club in the palm can also increase tension in the larger, slower muscles in the forearm... which will inhibit *Rotation* and decrease *Speed* in the movement.

Making sure the thumb and forefinger are on opposite sides of the grip/shaft is the last positional cue for promoting optimum Guiding Hand movement.

When the Guiding Hand thumb rests on top of the grip/shaft it inhibits *rotation* of the forearms which often causes the Club Face to be left wide open at Impact. It can also cause issues in timing *Club Face Speed...* by "casting" the shaft at the start of the downswing. **If you want to position yourself to maximize power, minimize effort and increase consistency... match your Guiding Hand palm to the leading edge of the Club Face, place the grip in your Guiding Hand fingers and make sure the thumb and forefinger are on opposite sides of the grip.**

Guiding Hand Basic Element #2

Proper Pressure for Both Hands

Striving for a light grip pressure (3 to 5 on a scale of 1 to 10 with 10 being as tight as you can hold the club) will have powerful, positive effects on your swing.

- **Increased *Speed*** - Your swing has multiple hinges. The hands are the hinge that transmits all the power from the body movements to the Club Face. **If your grip is too tight, it is like a rusty hinge. Your body and arms can generate lots of *Speed* but, the *Speed* will not make it to the Club Face if your grip pressure is too tight.** Body and arms generate... hands transmit. Tight hands do not transmit or transmit very slowly.

- **Smoother Rhythm** - Good swings are always rhythmic. Some are slow, some are fast BUT good ones always have smooth, fluid transitions. Rhythm and fluidity are VERY difficult to achieve with tense hands. **Imagine trying to write your signature holding the pen as tightly as you possibly can.** Excess tension produces jerky, forced transitions not smooth fluid ones.

- **Better *Feel*** - Keeping pressure light and constant from swing to swing and from start to finish during each swing will make each swing *FEEL* similar. If you want *Release Zone* motion to repeat... the same grip pressure with every club for every swing from address to finish is a great cue to focus on.

- **Full *Release*** - If you want to minimize wide open face shots and maximize distance, allowing the Club Face to fully *Release* (*rotate*) after Impact is an Essential Key. A very light grip pressure makes this much easier to achieve.

- **Less Injuries** - Light grip pressure puts much less strain on the entire body especially the wrists, elbows, shoulders, neck and back.

A very important "Key" to remember for grip pressure (worth a second mention on this page) is to maintain even grip pressure throughout the entire swing.

Watch out for loosening your grip pressure (letting go of the club) at the top of the backswing. Also, keep an eye out for tightening your grip pressure at the start of the downswing or at Impact. **Any of these grip pressure changes happening during your swing can make it very challenging to repeat ideal *Club Face Impact Keys*.**

Sweet Spot Helpful Exercise

Make a fist as tight as you can (10 on a scale of 1 to 10) ...now rotate your forearm. Can you feel the strain?

Lighten the pressure (3 on a scale of 1 to 10). Now *rotate* the forearm. Feel the difference in the strain?

Now multiply that by a few thousand golf swings and it will be easy to understand why your body will thank you for using light grip pressure.

Light grip pressure also encourages more of a swinging motion and less of a hitting motion. Swinging is fluid, rhythmic and effortless. Hitting is tense, forced and very tough on muscles and joints. Sam Snead was a true swinger of the club. He used a VERY light grip pressure (2 to 3 on a scale of 1 to 10) and won tournaments well into his 60's.

Trusting light grip pressure is a big challenge at first. The tendency is to hold on tight for control and power.

Take your time and lower your grip pressure VERY gradually to allow your body time to adjust to the different feel. Changing grip pressure too quickly will have negative effects on your ability to trust your swing on the course.

Now that your Guiding Hand is placed in the correct position on the club with the correct pressure, let's examine how your Guiding Hand will move to promote optimum *Release Zone* movement of the Club Face.

The Guiding Hand Movement Big Four

Follow this Guiding Hand progression to groove ideal Release Zone movement for Your Swing:

1. Late *Rotation* - Fast and Full
2. *Speed* Timing - The Pendulum Effect
3. Width - Reach and Release
4. Arc Angle - Find your Hand Path for Control

Step #1 in the Guiding Hand Big Four Progression

Rotate Late

You may have noticed Guiding Hand/Club Face *Rotation* timing is a recurring theme.

The *Rotation* of the Guiding Hand/Club Face is one of THE most powerful "Direct Influences" on the quality of your Sweet Spot shots.

Completely understanding the effect Guiding Hand *Rotation* has throughout your swing will not only help you produce more quality shots, it will help you self-diagnose challenges more accurately than ever before.

In the downswing, the *Rotation* of the Guiding Hand *Releases* the Club Face which creates part of the whip that produces *Maximum Speed*.

When the Guiding Hand reaches the right thigh (or is directly under the right shoulder) is when the *Rotation* of the Club Face begins.

Correctly timing the *Rotation* of the Club Face (which starts here) with the *Maximum Speed* of the Club Face (which occurs just after impact) while the club is travelling Down the Line is what separates the Sweet Spot golfers from everyone else.

This is one of THE most critical "timing marks" in *your* swing. As with all "positions" in your swing... it is very important to remember that this "position" is just a part of the *motion* of your entire swing.

Practice "Snapshots" to develop your *feel* for correct and incorrect... but remember your hands should be *accelerating* to the target from this "position" and your body should be *rotating* to the target from this "position". **Stopping or slowing down once you have reached this "position' in your swing... is a recipe for big trouble.**

It will help to visualize the three directions of the Club Face Path to make sure you totally understand this crucial relationship.

- When the Guiding Hand/Club Face is moving *From the Inside* it is extending and *accelerating.*
- When the Guiding Hand/Club Face is moving *Down the Line* it is fully extended, travelling to the target and going *Maximum Speed.*
- When the Guiding Hand/Club Face is moving *Back to the Inside* it is retracting and slowing down.

Ideally you want to time the *Rotation* of the Guiding Hand to square the Club Face during the *Down the Line* portion of the Path.

This means your Guiding Hand will start squaring the Club Face at your right thigh as it continues to accelerate to the target. Then your Club Face will come to square when your Guiding Hand reaches your left thigh... this will create Maximum Impact/Ball Speed while the Club Face is moving to the target.

Take a few minutes and run through the visual of this sequence in your mind... your shots will thank you for it.

When we relate this to Positive Shaft Lean, the Guiding Hand will square to the target AFTER it passes the ball (opposite your left thigh) on the way to the target.

This will guarantee the hands are ahead of the ball at Impact... and give you the best chance of connecting the Sweet Spots with correct Shaft Lean.

If you rotate the Guiding Hand too soon... you *Release* the *Speed* before Impact, the Club Face begins travelling *Back to the Inside* before impact and the shaft starts leaning the wrong way (Negative Shaft Lean and added loft).

The later in the swing you leave the Guiding Hand *Rotation*, the longer the Club Face travels toward the target and continues to *accelerate*.

If you are not holding the club too tightly... it is extremely difficult to rotate the Guiding Hand too late.

The anatomy is not designed for the Guiding Hand palm to stay facing the target line too long. **(Try it!)**

Two simple Guiding Hand goals can bring your swing big improvement and successful results:

- **Maximum Speed *through* Impact**
- **Maximum Rotation *after* Impact**

It may seem like training the timing of these two keys would be an impossible task.

However, the weighting and design of the club and the natural movement patterns of your body... will help you to train and trust this pattern quickly.

Especially if you make sure to train it with lots of practice swings first (80% correct) before adding a ball to the equation.

This timing does not have to be perfect... consistently close to correct will still have you playing great golf.

Step #2 in the Guiding Hand Big Four Progression

Speed Timing

One of the main overall goals for your Effective swing is to achieve *Maximum Speed* of the Club Face immediately AFTER impact EVERY swing.

Correctly timed Speed maximizes distance, minimizes poor contact and makes the swinging movement as easy on the joints and muscles of the body as possible.

Incorrectly timed *Speed* causes more than just loss of distance. It also causes ground first contact, standing up/pulling up through Impact and can contribute to slices and hooks as well.

Imagine your arms as a swinging pendulum.

The top of the backswing is the start, Impact is the bottom and the top of the follow through is the end of the Pendulum swing.

Your Guiding Hand Arm is the swinging pendulum. *Maximum Speed* of the arm/hand should naturally occur at the bottom of the arc (just before Impact). The Club Face *Maximum Speed* is just after this.

If you force the *Speed* from the top... full *Speed* will be wasted before Impact.

The arms and the Club Face can only *accelerate* to *Maximum Speed* once... use the pendulum image to make sure it is timed correctly. Whether the pendulum swing is fast or slow depends on your capabilities but, the Maximum Speed of the Guiding Hand/arm should always be at the bottom of the arc.

The Pendulum Effect goal for your swing is to make sure the Guiding Hand/arm accelerates at the same rate as the Club Face at the start of the downswing.

It should also reach *Maximum Speed* at the bottom of the arc... and the Club Face should reach *Maximum Speed* just after the Guiding Hand/arm (once again for emphasis!).

The longer the Guiding Hand/arm and Club Face match *acceleration* at the start of the downswing... the more power/*Speed* you retain for Impact, the better your Shaft Lean will be and the more efficient the contact with the ball is.

Developing an accurate sense of *acceleration/Speed* for the Club Face, the Guiding Hand/Arm and the body at the start of the downswing can be very challenging... especially if you are trying to monitor all three when you are swinging at a ball.

Eventually you *will* need to be able to *Feel* the difference between the correct and incorrect *acceleration/Speed* for all three parts during the transition... when you are hitting shots.

However, in the beginning... I would highly recommend doing a LOT of practice swings in slow motion and with no golf ball to develop an accurate sense of *Feel* for the correct transition with all three parts starting at the same *Speed*.

The visual reference for this is the angle between the club shaft and your arm... or the hinge in your Guiding Hand wrist.

The term for this is *Lag*.

If you measure the time from when your Guiding Hand reaches the ball until when the Club Face reaches the ball... the longer the time gap, the more *Lag* you have and the more efficient your swing is (have you hear this before?)

Think of it as cracking the whip. The Club Face is the tip of the whip. Did you know when a whip cracks the tip is moving at the speed of sound (over 750mph)?

As I mentioned earlier... it is very important that you should not attempt to hold this hinge with force.

Holding the hinge with force by increasing grip pressure will cause issues with *squaring* the Club Face properly at Impact and leads to poor contact. You will tend to leave the face wide open and hit a lot of thin or topped shots.

Also, when you use muscular force to hold the hinge... you will then have to consciously *release* the hinge. This adds an extra timing key which makes swing repeatability very difficult to achieve.

The goal is to set the hinge (load the shaft) on the backswing and then ALLOW the hinge to release (unload the shaft) when the momentum of the swing dictates on the downswing.

Practice slow motion swings with a very light grip and you will feel the hinge releasing itself.

This will also happen when you are swinging *Full Speed* with a ball... if your grip pressure is correct and you are not "throwing" away (casting) the hinge before it *Releases* itself.

Sweet Spot Concept Retention –

By the way... you may have noticed that I mention some principles in this book multiple times and in multiple sections. This is by design... multiple explanations of a concept will create a much higher chance of accurate retention.

Casting versus LAG at the start of the downswing is a BIG Sweet Spot "Key" so it gets extra attention.

If the Club Face out *accelerates* the Guiding Hand/arm at the beginning of the downswing, it causes the arm to decelerate through Impact, robbing you of Club Face Speed at Impact AND making correct Shaft Lean impossible.

Swinging the pendulum while retaining the hinge is a matter of "setting and forgetting" the angle.

Set the hinge on the backswing and it will stay there if you do not actively throw it away with your Guiding Hand... as the pendulum starts down. This is much like the *rotation* of the forearms/Club Face we discussed earlier.

This does not require strength... it just requires retraining the mind and muscles to swing the Guiding Hand and let the Club Face catch up as late as possible.

Golfers that are not super strong often have some of the most impressive lag/angle retention because they are not strong enough to "throw away" the hinge.

Grooving Guiding Hand *Rotation* and *Acceleration*

One Handed Swings

The most effective way to develop a feel for correct *rotation* and *acceleration* of the Guiding Hand is to isolate the hand, arm and club.

If you attempt to train pendulum *acceleration* and late *rotation* using a club and ball with both hands on the club... you will take more time than necessary to make the change effectively and permanently.

When creating new patterns, the less new information the brain takes in during each repetition... the better you can monitor the accuracy of your movement, the less incorrect repetitions you will make and the quicker you will be able to make effective change.

For more in depth help with changing old patterns, check out "Groove Your Move"... Book Two in my EvoYourSwing Instruction Series.

Hold a wedge in your Guiding Hand only.

Swing it to the top of the backswing (accuracy of the position at the top is not crucial).

When you swing down and through to the target, pay close attention to when the elbow and wrist unhinge, when your arm *rotates* the Club Face to square and when the arm reaches *Maximum Speed*.

Do not try to correct anything at first.

Awareness of right and wrong is step one to effective change. You must be able to "feel" right and wrong accurately before you can train your swing efficiently.

Isolating the movement to just the Guiding Hand, arm and club makes it much easier to accurately assess the quality of your movement.

It will not take long before you will notice a distinct snap movement at Impact... very much like the snap/*Release* of your wrist when you throw a ball.

You will also notice much more extension after Impact of your Guiding Hand/arm "to the target"... than you may be used to.

Correctly timing the *Rotation* of the Guiding Hand and the *Speed* of the Guiding Hand will make your swing feel more like a throwing/swinging motion and less like a hitting motion.

As you get more comfortable with this feel, you can think about swinging with a ball in the equation with one arm only. You will want to tee the ball slightly and use your favorite iron.

You may find your club striking the ground before Impact when you first begin using a ball. This is not unusual. Many golfers Guiding Hands are patterned to *rotate*, extend the arm and accelerate the Club Face too early in the downswing... and it will take some repetitions before the correct timing for the snap/release kicks in.

One handed Guiding Hand swings are one of the most powerful tools in building your Sweet Spot swing.

I have seen several PGA Tour Pros using one handed Guiding Hand practice swings on the range on a consistent basis.

If you have limited time to practice and play... I would highly recommend focusing all your energy on integrating Late *Rotation* and The Pendulum Effect for *Speed* into your swing.

As with Late Club Face Rotation and Timed Club Face Speed in the Release Zone... these two elements of the Guiding Hand Big Four produce the most dramatic results in the shortest time.

My students have experienced amazing results applying these concepts to their *essential swing movements* training.

If you are seeking the highest levels of skill and the lowest scores on your score card... then let's check out the last two of the Guiding Hand Big Four.

Because parts of these two elements are outside of the *Release Zone*... they do not have as much of a "Direct Influence" on the quality of your shots. But they are still very helpful tools in your quest for Sweet Spot Shots.

Step #3 in the Guiding Hand Big Four Progression

Width

Width is a very popular concept in golf especially when discussing power... and one that is discussed at length in my EvoYourSwing Series Book Three "The Power Primer" and in my Sweet Spot Shots Video Lessons.

The theory... a wider swing Arc can produce more power.

The reality... it is the correct blend of your Guiding Hand Arc and Club Face Arc in the downswing (lag) that will produce more *Speed* and power.

A word of caution... a wider Arc of just your Club Face at the start of the downswing (casting) can ruin any chance you have of creating power.

Make sure you fully understand the difference between width of the Guiding Hand Arc and the width of the Club Face Arc. The Guiding Hand width will be determined by the length of your front arm (in my case the left arm). In the downswing... the goal is to keep the arc width of both arcs constant as far into the downswing as possible. The most common is the Club Face Arc getting too wide at the start of the downswing. **ALL Sweet Spot swings have the proper blend of these two Arcs.**

136

The three key areas for Arc Width are:

1. Finish of the Back Swing
2. Start of the Down Swing
3. Halfway into the Follow Through.

Finish of the Backswing Width

Reach and Resist

One of the most effective ways to create power and consistency during your backswing is to create as much width as the strength in your lower body and the flexibility in your upper body will allow.

Resisting with your legs throughout the backswing and stretching with your Guiding Hand creates a tremendous coil in your body which allows you to minimize the size of your back swing and maximize the *Speed* in your downswing. **Visualize it as stretching a rubber band as fully as possible.**

The lower body acts like the thumb you place the rubber band on... and the Guiding Hand is the fingers of the other hand that stretches the rubber band. The muscles in your shoulders, core and upper legs are the rubber band.

The more stretch/coil you create on the way back, the less effort it takes to create *Speed* on the way toward the target.

If you imagine stretching the rubber band fully and aiming it as the backswing... the downswing becomes a simple release, just letting the rubber band go to the target.

If you do not resist (minimize rotation) from the waist down in the backswing you will not create optimal coil in the legs and core no matter how long the back swing is. Your backswing can also become so long it is difficult to control.

If you do not maintain the width of your Guiding Hand (keep it as far from your head as possible) you will lose the coil in your back, shoulders and upper arm. This is often seen as the front arm (left arm for right handed golfers) collapsing or bending.

Maintaining the width and keeping the front arm long is much easier to accomplish if you focus on the Guiding Hand helping you to full stretch.

Try it!

Hold the club with just your front arm (left arm for right handed golfers) and try to maintain width to the top, then add the Guiding Hand and use it to stretch the front arm to the top. You will notice a lot more width at the top with the help of the Guiding Hand.

Width is mostly associated with power generation and *Speed* but, maintaining ideal width throughout the swing is also a huge help in creating a repeating Club Face motion in the *Release Zone*.

When the Arc of the Club Face changes size at the wrong time or too often you may struggle with contact... a constant Arc makes it much easier to *Scuff* the ground in the same place consistently.

When the Guiding Hand Arc loses width at the top of the backswing or extends too soon in the downswing you will lose power because the *Speed* of the Club Face will be incorrectly timed.

Sweet Spot Helpful Hint –

If you have flexibility issues or health concerns about your lower back, hips or shoulders... be careful about the amount of coil you try to create in your backswing.

Coil is powerful... but it does add a lot of torsion to your muscles. Use good judgement to make sure your swing allows you to play as much as possible and avoid pain and injury at all costs.

Start of the Down Swing Width

Transition Speeds and Casting

Once you have coiled properly on the way back, maintaining ideal width of your Guiding Hand and Club Face during the start of the down swing is the next step to creating ideal *Release Zone* movement. This is the area of the swing where it is critical to know the difference between width of the Guiding Hand Arc and the width of the Club Face Arc.

A Sweet Spot swing transition happens when your Guiding Hand and Club Face downswing Arcs come as close as possible to matching the width and hinge angle of their backswing Arcs... until it is time to *Release* the Club Face in the *Release Zone*.

140

Both downswing Arcs will be narrower (because of the body rotation bringing the arms in closer to the body) but, striving for equal width and *hinge retention* is an effective training tool.

Hinge retention is about Speed... not force.

If your hands/arms are moving the same *Speed* as the Club Face until waist high... then the hinge will be maintained until waist high.

Matching the Speed of your body rotation to the Speed of the Club Face and your hands/arms is a good cue for getting your downswing starting correctly and maintaining good width.

It is only when the Club Face travels faster than the hands/arms that the hinge is lost.

Only the muscles in your Guiding Hand, wrist and forearm can cause the Club Face to move too fast too soon. Raise your awareness of the *Speed* of the Club Face versus the *Speed* of your hands/arms and you will have a much better chance of saving *Full Speed* for Impact and swinging with ideal width in the transition. **Correct *Speed* Timing in the transition is also the cure for casting... which is widening the Arc of the Club Face at the start of the downswing.**

Speed Timing is the feel "component" and casting is the visual "component" of this common and troublesome transition flaw.

When you cast during the transition, you widen the Club Face Arc too soon... which causes an early release of *Speed* and loss of the hinge.

Poor contact, poor direction and loss of power are direct results of casting/poor *Speed* timing.

These transition issues are a multi-headed monster that are THE biggest causes of poor golf shots... outside of *Release Zone* issues.

Training your Sweet Spot swing to have maximum Guiding Hand width and correct Club Face width (and *Speed*) during the transition is crucial.

Maintaining the correct width and *Speed* as far into the downswing as possible is one of the biggest positive changes you can make on your swing... outside of the *Release Zone*.

If you can also train your Guiding Hand to NOT throw away the hinge, it will make generating *Speed* and squaring the face during the *Release Zone* much easier and more of a reflex action... as opposed to a controlled action.

Half Way into the Follow Through Width

Release to the Target

Look at pictures of tour pros halfway into the follow through and you will ALWAYS see their Guiding Hand fully extending the Arc to the target.

When both hands reach waist high on the follow through they should be at maximum distance from your head and parallel to the target line. The Guiding Hand palm should also be parallel to the target line.

This position is the end of the *Release Zone* and gives you a very accurate indicator of the quality of your swing... and the probability of your shot hitting the target.

The simplest image for proper Guiding Hand width throughout your swing is to visualize your Guiding Hand tracking in a constant Arc as far away from your head as your body can support. The Arc your hands travel through will vary slightly at different parts of the swing (narrower half way into the downswing, wider halfway into the follow through) but focusing on maintaining width throughout the swing is a good cue for building power and consistency into your Sweet Spot swing.

Your swing will feel a lot more stretched than you are used to... especially at the top of the backswing but, the power and repeatability will make the change well worth your while.

- **Stretch on the way back. *Release* on the way through.**
- **Wind up wide. Unwind wide. Follow through wide.**
- **Your swing will generate power and consistency effortlessly.**

Grooving Guiding Hand Width

The Mirror

A full-length mirror is one of the easiest ways to imprint the visual cues of new swing movements into your brain and a great tool for speeding the improvement process.

Stand facing the mirror and far enough away so you can see your entire body throughout the swing. You can use a full-length club if your ceilings are high enough or you can cut down an old club to minimize paint and spackle repairs.

You are monitoring three things while watching yourself swing:

- **Keeping your Guiding Hand as far from your head as your body can support throughout the swing.**
- **Keeping your head as centered as possible throughout the swing.**
- **The Guiding Hand wrist and elbow hinges are retained from the top to the back swing to the start of the Release Zone.**

Start VERY, VERY slowly and gradually increase *Speed* until you can monitor accurately even at normal *Speed*.

Follow this with "eyes closed" swings to get your feel to match the new visual.

<u>Step #4 of the Guiding Hand Big Four Progression</u>

Guiding Hand Arc Angle

Understanding and training the optimum Guiding Hand Arc Angle (Hand Path) for YOU is one of the biggest influences (outside of the *Release Zone*) on your ability to create consistent *Down the Line* Face Path at Impact with every club.

The goal is to swing your Guiding Hand back and through on the same Arc... AND for that Arc to make it as easy as possible for YOU to achieve optimum *Release Zone* movements.

When your Guiding Hand Arc (Hand Path) is on an effective and matching plane for backswing and downswing:

- *Down the Line Path* is easier to achieve
- Late *Face Rotation* takes less effort
- Ideal *Scuff* is simpler to repeat
- Consistency in all areas improves

When the Guiding Hand swings too vertically/upright it will tend to cause the *Release Zone* Movement to be too steep.

This means the *Scuff* point gets very short and very deep, making consistent Sweet Spot contact difficult to achieve.

The resulting swings would tend to produce heavy club head contact with the ground before the ball... or contact with the top half of the ball.

It also makes ideal Club Face rotation more challenging since rotation takes more effort on a steeper Guiding Hand Arc (Hand Path).

Here are other potential issues with a Guiding Hand Arc that is too upright:

- The Club Face tends to move *Back to the Inside* too early in the *Release Zone*, producing pulls to the left and slices to the right depending on Club Face Aim.
- The arms tend to swing separate from the body which creates timing issues and allows the backswing to get excessively long.
- The balance point in your feet moves too far toward the toes causing stance instability... especially on uneven lies.

To make an upright (steep) Guiding Hand Arc work, your Guiding Hand would have to actively flatten the club shaft during the down swing.

This is an extra step to be avoided if possible.

A good rule of thumb is... any extra steps or extra movements should be eliminated from your swing whenever possible.

Extra moving parts mean the potential for consistency is drastically reduced and the amount of maintenance required to keep *your* swing tuned increases significantly.

As a teacher... I believe you already have a great golf swing inside your body and your mind.

My job is to help you "peel away" the extra "stuff" to get to the great swing inside... and do it faster than you could do on your own.

This book is a descriptive and visual tool designed to help in the "peeling" process.

The simplest swings that use the least amount of effort are my favorite swings to watch and to teach.

Sweet Spot Mantras

Effortless Power... not Powerless Effort

Increase Simplicity... decrease Frustration

Fewer Thoughts... more Sweet Spot Shots

When the Guiding Hand swings too horizontal/flat you will have a too shallow Club Face Impact and have direction control issues with your shots.

A too flat (shallow) Guiding Hand Arc does not stay on the target line long enough at Impact for the Club Face to consistently square at the correct time... while it is travelling *Down the Line*.

A flat Guiding Hand Arc also promotes excessive rotation of the Club Face in the *Release Zone*. It can also cause the upper body to rotate too quickly in the downswing. This would cause the Club Face to move left of the target line too soon in the downswing (*Back to the Inside*).

151

Here are other potential issues with a Guiding Hand Arc that is too flat:

- Because the flat arc does not allow the face to travel *Down the Line* very long at Impact, slight changes in tempo, rhythm and grip pressure can create very different Club Face Aim and Club Paths at Impact.
- The result is that your shots can fly in a wide dispersion pattern... making accurate targeting nearly impossible.
- The flat/shallow arc can also cause early ground scuffs or thin contact especially with the longer clubs.

Finding the correct Guiding Hand Arc angle for YOU will help you avoid a lot of frustration in the improvement process.

The "Just Right" Guiding Hand Arc tracks from your set up position to a spot where your Guiding Hand is in line with your heel or the back of your Guiding Hand shoulder.

This Guiding Hand Arc will help create a *Down the Line Club Face Path* and Vertical Arc (*Scuff*) that gives you the best chance for optimum *Release Zone* movement, Sweet Spot contact and *Sweet Spot Shots*. Since every golfer is built differently, there is no perfect Guiding Hand Arc for everyone. Check out the picture to see the window where you can effectively place your hands at the top of the back swing.

Sweet Spot Helpful Hint

When tracking Hand Path... raise your awareness of how close your Guiding Hand is to your right thigh as it approaches Impact. Closer is better! Too far away causes *Back to the Inside Path*.

Grooving Guiding Hand Arc Angle

The Mirror

The guiding Hand Arc is best viewed in the mirror from a *Down the Line* perspective.

When in your setup position make note of where your Guiding Hand is in the mirror. You might even want to have a friend make a mark on the mirror to show hand position.

Bring the club to the top of your backswing. Your hands (or the butt of the club) should be roughly in line with your heels or the back of your right shoulder.

Here again we have three keys to monitor:

- **Make sure your hands are not too far forward of, or too far behind your heel line.**
- **Return your hands to their address position at Impact.**
- **Follow as direct an Arc from address to top of backswing and back to Impact as possible.**

One of the most common swing flaws is the downswing following a steeper (more vertical) Arc than the backswing (often called "coming over the top").

When you can swing with a clean, simple, effective Guiding Hand Arc with your eyes open or closed, with or without a club, you are ready to start applying your Sweet Spot Guiding Hand Arc swing to hitting shots at the range.

The Guiding Hand - Review and Goals

Hold the club in a Target facing/ neutral palm position

When your Guiding Hand arm hangs naturally from the shoulder, your palm will face the target.

If you place it on the club this way it will try to return to the correct position at Impact and make a full, well timed *Release* easier to accomplish.

Let the natural movement patterns of your body help you create repeating *Release Zone* optimum *squaring* of the Club Face.

Hold the club lightly in the fingers to promote speed. *Speed* without effort is always a worthwhile goal in golf. *Speed* produces distance. The muscles in your fingers are much faster twitch muscles than those in the palm and forearm.

Hold the club lightly in the fingers to reduce effort. Minimizing effort aids consistency and reduces strain on joints and muscles.

If you want strength for hitting something hard... hold the club in the palm with a tight grip pressure.

If you want more distance with an easier swing... hold the club lightly in the fingers of your Guiding Hand.

Rotate the Guiding Hand to square as late as possible before Impact

If you swing your Guiding Hand arm without a club it will *rotate* when the right hand passes underneath the right shoulder (Try it!).

This also happens to be the perfect timing for *Rotating* the Club Face to square it as late and consistently as possible.

Why not let your natural body movement's help you hit more consistent and powerful Sweet Spot shots?

Focus on a Pendulum swing with *Maximum Speed* at the bottom of the arc

It is critically important to time your Speed correctly.

Whether you start your downswing with your legs, hips, core or arms... make sure the *Speed* of your Guiding Hand is reaching its peak in the middle of the *Release Zone*.

Your Club Face *Maximum Speed* will happen just after your Guiding Hand reaches *Maximum Speed*... due to Lag

For most full swings, you should also strive to max out at 80-85% of your potential *Full Speed*. Attempting to swing at 100% of *Full Speed* on a regular basis is a recipe for inconsistency, out of control shots and an overly strained body. Imagine a pitcher throwing every pitch as hard as possible.

Strive for Guiding Hand Arc Width

The wider the Arc of your Guiding Hand the more potential your swing has for power AND consistency. A longer Arc can also increase power but, it can reduce consistency. A longer Arc is also much more likely to cause *Speed Timing* and Club Face *Release Timing* issues.

Keep the Arc wide, the swing compact and centered ... and you will hit more powerful shots for a long time to come.

Find YOUR best Guiding Hand Arc Angle

Training an optimum Guiding Hand Arc angle for you is one of the simplest ways to create correct shaft plane, Down the Line Impact and great balance in your swing.

 Slightly steep or slightly flat will work just fine if it is comfortable for your body, the club approaches the *Release Zone* correctly and the backswing and downswing track match each other. Excessively different backswing and downswing Arcs make consistency much more difficult to achieve without multiple corrections and manipulations each swing.

Finding an Arc angle that matches your body and swing style will make you wonder how you ever swung the club any other way.

The Guiding Hand is the closest part of your body to the Club Face... which is the only Direct Influence on the flight of your golf shots. Use your most dexterous and easily trained body part to connect you to the Club Face ...and you will connect the Sweet Spots more consistently and hit a lot more targets.

Training your swing using the Guiding Hand is the simplest way to dramatically increase your golfing skill in the shortest amount of time.

You may or may not find the Guiding Hand to be an effective cue for when you are hitting shots on the golf course.

I have students who perform best using shoulder cues, arm cues, core cues, hip cues and even leg cues. But, making changes in your swing is accomplished fastest using the Guiding Hand.

The biggest challenge when making changes... is developing accurate feel for the difference between correct and incorrect.

Using a very sensitive and familiar part of the body to help raise awareness not only makes sense... it works.

Another "Key" to making effective change... is to perform the *correct* repetitions *consistently.* Old patterns will not change if your repetitions are of poor quality or intermittent consistency (daily is best... even if they are just visualizations of the new movement).

THE SWEET SPOT REVIEW

Improving your golf swing can be a Simple and Successful process.

Train your Path... Train your Loft... Train your Aim... and you will hit better shots and play better golf.

The Club Face is the only Direct Influence on the golf ball flight to the target.

Swing the Sweet Spot of the Club Face through the Sweet Spot of the Ball when the Club Face is moving toward the target.

Time the *Speed* of the Club Face and the *Rotation* of the Club Face correctly and you will dramatically increase control, consistency and power.

Your Guiding Hand is THE most "Direct Influence" on the Club Face. Train your Guiding Hand and it will give you a strong awareness of right and wrong with the Club Face movement.

Create a crystal-clear *picture* in your mind of your goals.

Practice the relevant drills without a ball until you can *feel* the correct movement.

When you can perform consistently at the range without thinking during the swing... then it is time to bring your new movements to the course.

If you are struggling in your change process... "Reduce to Produce" or use the "Opposite Fix".

If you enjoyed the content and presentation of The Sweet Spot please take a few minutes and write a positive review of the book on Amazon.

My passion is to help as many golfers as possible... and positive reviews encourage more people to read the book and experience the enjoyment of hitting more Sweet Spot Shots.

Make sure to check out my other two books in the EvoYourSwing Instruction Series: "Groove Your Move" and "The Power Primer"

If you enjoyed the principles of this book, but would prefer an in-depth video lesson format... I have produced a complete 30 lesson (over 5 hours) instruction series called "Sweet Spot Shots" on Amazon Video Direct. It contains all my best tips, training and mental game strategies in a 5 season, step by step program.

Please feel free to contact me at:

geoff@evoswinggolf.com

ABOUT THE AUTHOR

Geoff has over 20 years of golf teaching experience including Teaching Professional at Torrey Pines Golf Course, Regional Director for the Nike Golf Learning Centers, Teaching Professional at the Green Valley Ranch Academy and Teaching Professional at Common Ground Golf Course. He has taught over 15,000 lessons and learned invaluable insights from this diverse student database on how to apply his golf knowledge to help each student progress on their own individual path.

Geoff also has an extensive background teaching movement skills in several sports including: soccer, Tai Chi, skiing and fitness... in addition to golf. His unique multi-sport background combined with his highly- developed communication skills means that golfers from all backgrounds, all levels of skill and all learning styles have experienced rapid improvement and lasting results.

Before his teaching career, Geoff played golf professionally on two different golf mini tours, played professional soccer in the US and England, ski raced in college and was inducted in to the University of Vermont Athletic Hall of Fame. His successes, struggles and wide variety of experiences give him a unique perspective on sports performance improvement.

AWARDS

1995 Inducted into the University of Vermont Athletic Hall of Fame

2000 Colorado PGA Section Professional of the Month

2000 American Golf Professional of the Year for the Western US

2005 PGA President's Council Growth of the Game Award

2013 Amazon Best Selling Book (The Sweet Spot)

2013 Amazon Best Selling Author

2015 Colorado Avid Golfer Award - Best Mental Game Instructor

2016 Colorado Avid Golfer Award - Staff Pick Best Instructor

Made in the USA
San Bernardino, CA
16 March 2017